Understanding Game Application Development

With Xamarin.Forms and ASP.NET

Vincent Maverick S. Durano

Apress®

Understanding Game Application Development

Vincent Maverick S. Durano
Minnetonka, MN, USA

ISBN-13 (pbk): 978-1-4842-4263-6 ISBN-13 (electronic): 978-1-4842-4264-3
https://doi.org/10.1007/978-1-4842-4264-3

Library of Congress Control Number: 2018966347

Managing Director, Apress Media LLC: Welmoed Spahr
Acquisitions Editor: Smriti Srivastava
Development Editor: Matthew Moodie
Coordinating Editor: Shrikant Vishwakarma

Cover designed by eStudioCalamar

Cover image designed by Freepik (www.freepik.com)

Distributed to the book trade worldwide by Springer Science+Business Media New York, 233 Spring Street, 6th Floor, New York, NY 10013. Phone 1-800-SPRINGER, fax (201) 348-4505, e-mail orders-ny@springer-sbm.com, or visit www.springeronline.com. Apress Media, LLC is a California LLC and the sole member (owner) is Springer Science + Business Media Finance Inc (SSBM Finance Inc). SSBM Finance Inc is a **Delaware** corporation.

For information on translations, please e-mail rights@apress.com, or visit http://www.apress.com/rights-permissions.

Apress titles may be purchased in bulk for academic, corporate, or promotional use. eBook versions and licenses are also available for most titles. For more information, reference our Print and eBook Bulk Sales web page at http://www.apress.com/bulk-sales.

Any source code or other supplementary material referenced by the author in this book is available to readers on GitHub via the book's product page, located at www.apress.com/978-1-4842-4263-6. For more detailed information, please visit http://www.apress.com/source-code.

Printed on acid-free paper

I dedicate this book to my kids: Vianne Maverich Durano and Vynn Markus Durano.

To my wife, Michelle Anne, who's always accepted me as I am and supported my hustle, drive, and ambition: you are and always will be my perfect wife and mother to our children. I love you!

To my mom, Lilibeth: There are no words that can express how I feel, and I'll always thank the Lord you made me. I love you, Mom. You are appreciated.

To my Aunt Veronica and my grandparents, Papa Daddy and Mama Nieves: There's NO way I can pay you back, and I'll never fully understand, but I want you to know YOU raised a good man.

To my sister, Angel Cristine, and to the rest of my family back in the Philippines: Thank you so much for being supportive.

To all my friends, especially Daniel De Leon: Thank you for being supportive. I truly appreciate all your kindness.

Finally, to all my article readers and followers: Thank you so much for your support and for giving me the motivation to contribute more in the technical community. You all are my energy to keep me going. Thank you!

Table of Contents

About the Author

Vincent Maverick S. Durano is a proud Cebuano. He's originally from the Philippines and now works as a Solutions Architect / Senior Software Engineer in a research and development company based in USA, focusing mainly on web and mobile technologies. He is a nine-time Microsoft MVP, three-time C# Corner MVP, CodeProject MVP, Microsoft Influencer, DZone MVB, and a regular contributor at CodeProject, CsharpCorner, Microsoft TechNet Wiki, AspSnippets, and Xamarin. He also contributes at the official Microsoft ASP.NET community site, where he became one of the all-time top answerers with All-Star recognition level (the highest attainable level).

He has authored e-books for C# Corner, including *GridView Control Pocket Guide,* Dockerizing ASP.NET Core and Blazor Applications on Mac and *ASP.NET MVC 5: A Beginner's Guide,* and is now working on a new book entitled *ASP.NET Core 2: A Beginner's Guide.*

He runs a blog at `http://vmsdurano.com` and has created a few open source projects that are hosted on Codeplex and GitHub. He also developed the VMD.RESTApiResponseWrapper.Core and VMD.RESTApiResponseWrapper.Net NuGet packages.

About the Technical Reviewers

Afzaal Ahmad Zeeshan is a computer programmer from Rabwah, Pakistan; he likes .NET Core for regular day development and has experience with Cloud, Mobile, and API development. Afzaal Ahmad has experience with the Azure platform and likes to build cross-platform libraries/software with .NET Core. He has been recognized as a Microsoft MVP for his work in the field of software development and as a CodeProject MVP and C# Corner MVP for technical writing and mentoring.

Syed Shanu is a three-time Microsoft MVP, a four-time C# Corner MVP, and a four-time Code project MVP. Shanu is also an author, blogger, and speaker. He's from Madurai, Tamil Nadu, India, and works as Technical Lead in South Korea. With more than 11 years of experience with Microsoft technologies, Shanu is an active person in the community and is always happy to share his knowledge on topics related to ASP.NET, MVC, ASP.NET Core, Web API, SQL Server, Angular, and ASP.NET Core Blazor, among others. He has written more than 100 articles on various technologies. He's also a several-time TechNet Guru Gold Winner. Follow him on Twitter @syedshanu3.

Introduction

Technologies are constantly evolving, and as .NET developers we need to cope with the latest or at least with what's popular nowadays. At the beginning, you might find yourself having a hard time catching up with the latest technologies due to confusion about what sets of technologies to use and where to start. There are tons of resources out there that you can use as a reference to learn, but you still find it hard to connect the dots in the picture. Sometimes you might even think of losing the interest to learn and giving up. If you are confused and have no idea how to start building an iOS or Android mobile application from scratch and how to connect your app with your database and API, then this book is for you.

Keep in mind that this book highlights only the basic implementation of a mind/memory game type of mobile application. If you are looking for an action, adventure, card, RPG, or sports type of game app development, then this book is not for you.

Understanding Game Development with Xamarin.Forms and ASP.NET will walk you through how to build a simple data-driven mobile game application using the power of Xamarin.Forms and Web API. We will also build a real-time leaderboard page using ASP.NET MVC and SignalR.

This book covers topics from creating a SQL database from scratch, to building the Web API endpoints, to making a mobile application that targets both iOS and Android, to building a real-time leaderboard page for player rankings, deployment, and testing, and finally down to publishing your code to GitHub.

The goal of this book is to guide .NET developers who might become interested in mobile application development if they discover the need for a simple working game application that requires some kind of feature that connects data from a mobile app to other services such as a REST application or a web application.

This book is targeted for beginners to intermediate .NET developers who want to jump into mobile application development with Xamarin and get their hands dirty with practical examples.

I've written this book so that it's easy to follow and understand by providing step-by-step processes with as many detailed code explanations as possible. As you go along to the end of the book, you will learn the basic concepts and fundamentals of each of the technologies used for building the whole application and how they connect to each other.

CHAPTER 1

Introduction

Technologies are constantly evolving, and as .NET developers we need to cope with the latest or at least what's popular nowadays. At the beginning, you might find yourself having a hard time catching up with the newest technologies due to confusion about what sets of technologies to use and where to start. There are tons of resources out there that you can use as a reference to learn, but you still find it hard to connect the dots in the picture. Sometimes you might even think of losing the interest to learn and giving up. If you are confused and have no idea how to start building an iOS or Android mobile application from scratch and how to connect your app with your database and API, then this book is for you.

Keep in mind that this book highlights only the basic implementation of a mind/memory game type of mobile application. If you are looking for an action, adventure, card, RPG, or sports type of game app development, then this book is not for you.

This book, *Understanding Game Application Development with Xamarin.Forms and ASP.NET*, will walk you through how to build a simple data-driven mobile game application using the power of Xamarin and Web API. We will also build a real-time leaderboard page using ASP.NET model-view-controller (MVC) and SignalR.

This book covers topics from creating a SQL database from scratch, to building the Web API endpoints, to making a mobile application that targets both iOS and Android, to building a real-time leaderboard page for player rankings, and finally down to deployment.

V. M. S. Durano, *Understanding Game Application Development*,
https://doi.org/10.1007/978-1-4842-4264-3_1

The goal of this book is to guide .NET developers who might become interested in mobile application development if they discover the need for a simple working game application that requires some kind of feature that connects data from a mobile app to other services such as a REST application or a web application.

This book is targeted for beginners to intermediate .NET developers who want to jump on mobile application development with Xamarin and get their hands dirty with practical examples.

I've written this book so that it's easy to follow and understand by providing step-by-step processes with as many detailed code explanations as possible. As you go along to the end of the book, you will learn the basic concepts and fundamentals of each of the technologies used for building the whole application and how each of them connects to each other.

Roadmap

Chapter 1

Chapter 1 presents an overview of who this book is for and a short backgrounder about which sets of technologies will be used to build the web and mobile applications as well as why we choose to use them. It also gives a brief overview of "Working Memory," which is the type of game application that this book is going to cover. This chapter highlights the topics of what the reader will learn from the book. It also highlights a brief overview of Xamarin.Forms, ASP.NET Web API, MVC, SignalR, and Entity Framework (EF) and discusses how to connect them all together to achieve a goal. It also talks about the required tools and framework needed to build the application as well as provides instructions on how to configure and install them on your development machine.

Chapter 2

Chapter 2 provides a game overview and discusses application flow, creating and running the core mobile application projects using Xamarin. Forms, and installing the required NuGet packages for the applications. The application flow section discusses the process by which the system handles the requests from one application layer to another starting from account creation/login down to playing the game, syncing data in real time, and ultimately persisting the changes in the database. The game overview section deals with the mechanics and objective of the game.

Chapter 3

Chapter 3 contains information about data access configuration using EF as well as building REST API endpoints using ASP.NET Web API. The first section of this chapter discusses database creation. The second section describes the steps to integrate EF into the Web API project and then set up a data access layer for implementing create, read, update, and delete (CRUD) operations. The third section of this chapter considers the creation of REST API endpoints, how to enable cross-origin resource sharing (CORS), and finally how to test the endpoints.

Chapter 4

Chapter 4 contains the actual implementation of the mobile application using Xamarin.Forms. This chapter is the core of the book, as it discusses the detailed steps and procedures for building the Working Memory game application targeting both Android and iOS platforms. The step-by-step procedure and breaking the code into sections with explanations should give readers a better understanding of how the application works.

Chapter 5

Chapter 5 discusses building a real-time leaderboard page using ASP.NET MVC and SignalR, with a detailed explanation of how real-time communication works for the project.

Chapter 6

Chapter 6 discusses the steps and procedures for how to deploy and test the mobile apps in platform-specific device emulators using the Conveyor plug-in and the SharpProxy tool.

Chapter 7

Chapter 7 walks you through how to push your application code to GitHub using Visual Studio 2017, and it also contains the source code link and resource references used in this book.

Background

Years ago, I was tasked to create a proof-of-concept application about "Working Memory" in a form of a mobile app game and at the same time provide a web app that displays leaderboard. I was a bit nervous and at the same time curious about it, since building a mobile application isn't really my area of expertise. Having the opportunity to work with mobile applications, particularly game development, is very exciting, as this is getting more popular nowadays. Building mobile apps or even wearable apps is not as complex as you may think. Using the right tools and technologies makes life easier for us to build mobile apps and prototypes.

Ermm..., the right tools and technologies?

Yes! Specifically, I am referring to the awesome Xamarin.

Xamarin allows you to build cross-platform apps for Android, iOS, and UWP, and it uses C# as the back-end language. Xamarin also introduced Xamarin.Forms, which allows you to easily create native user interface (UI) layouts that can be shared across Android, iOS, and Windows phones. As long as you know C#, creating the logic for your app is easy because you will already be familiar with the syntax and most of all the .NET libraries. The only learning curve when transitioning from web to mobile is that you will need to know and understand how Android, iOS, and Windows platforms work and how each framework interprets stuff. I have decided to use Xamarin, ASP.NET, and Visual Studio for the following reasons:

- Xamarin is now fully integrated with the latest Visual Studio release (VS 2017 as of this time of writing).
- Xamarin allows you to build cross-platform apps (iOS, Android, and UWP) using C#.
- I am an experienced C# developer.
- I am an experienced ASP.NET developer.
- I am more familiar with Visual Studio development tools.
- I don't need to learn how to use other frameworks, editors, tools, or programming languages to build native apps.
- I can take advantage of the cool features provided by Xamarin, such as cloud testing and app monitoring.
- Xamarin and Visual Studio are quite popular and stable platforms for building real-world apps.
- Xamarin has its own dedicated support site, so when you encounter any problem during your development, you can easily post your query to their dedicated forums.

I'm writing this book so anyone interested in mobile application development can refer to it if they need a simple working game application that requires features that connect data from a mobile app to other services such as a REST application or web application. This book will walk you through on building a simple Working Memory game application using the power of Xamarin and ASP.NET.

Before we dig down further, let's talk a bit about Working Memory.

WHAT IS WORKING MEMORY?

According to the documentation, Working Memory is a cognitive system with a limited capacity that is responsible for temporarily holding information available for processing. Working Memory is important for reasoning and the guidance of decision-making and behavior. We can say that Working Memory is a crucial brain function that we use to focus our attention and control our thinking. For more information, please see the References section at the end of this book.

What You Will Learn

This book is targeted for beginners to intermediate .NET developers who want to build a data-driven mobile application that connects to other services from scratch and get their hands dirty with practical examples. I've written this book to be easy to follow and understand. As you go along to the end, you will learn the following:

- The basic concepts and fundamentals of the relevant technologies used for building entire applications.
- How to download and install the required tools and development framework.

- How to set up a SQL Server database from scratch.
- How to build a simple Working Memory game application using Xamarin.Forms that targets both iOS and Android platforms.
- How to create an ASP.NET Web API project.
- How to integrate EF as our data access mechanism.
- How to create an ASP.NET MVC 5 project.
- How to integrate ASP.NET SignalR within the ASP.NET MVC application.
- How to invoke a SignalR Hub client proxy from a Web API project.
- Deploying and testing the applications in platform-specific device emulators.
- Pushing your code to GitHub using Visual Studio 2017.

Prerequisites

Before you read any further, make sure that you have the necessary requirements for your system and that your development environment is properly configured. This demo uses the following platform and frameworks:

- Windows 10
- Visual Studio 2017
- SQL Server Express Edition 2017
- SQL Server Management Studio (SSMS) 17.9
- Xamarin 4.11

- ASP.NET Web API 2
- ASP.NET MVC 5
- ASP.NET SignalR 2.2
- EF 6

Basic knowledge of the following languages and concepts is also required:

- C#
- SQL
- JavaScript/jQuery
- AJAX
- HTML
- XAML (eXtensible Application Markup Language)
- HTTP Request and Response
- OOP

Development Tools Download Resources

You can download Visual Studio and SQL Server Express edition at the following links:

Windows

- `www.visualstudio.com/downloads/`
- `www.microsoft.com/en-us/sql-server/sql-server-editions-express`

Mac

- `https://code.visualstudio.com/download`
- `www.visualstudio.com/downloads/` (Visual Studio for Mac)
- `https://database.guide/how-to-install-sql-server-on-a-mac/`

Installation Guide

For this demo, I'm going to develop the application on a Windows 10 machine, as I am more familiar and comfortable building .NET applications in a Windows environment. If you are on Mac, then follow the download link mentioned in the preceding "Development Tools Download Resources" section.

Visual Studio 2017

Microsoft Visual Studio is an integrated development environment (IDE) from Microsoft. It is used to develop computer programs as well as websites, web apps, web services, and mobile apps. The latest version of Visual Studio is now a full-featured IDE for Android, iOS, Windows, web, and cloud, which makes it a comfortable and powerful choice for building applications in the context of .NET.

Let's go ahead and download Visual Studio via this link: `https://visualstudio.microsoft.com/downloads/`. Once you land on the download link, you should be presented with the following page:

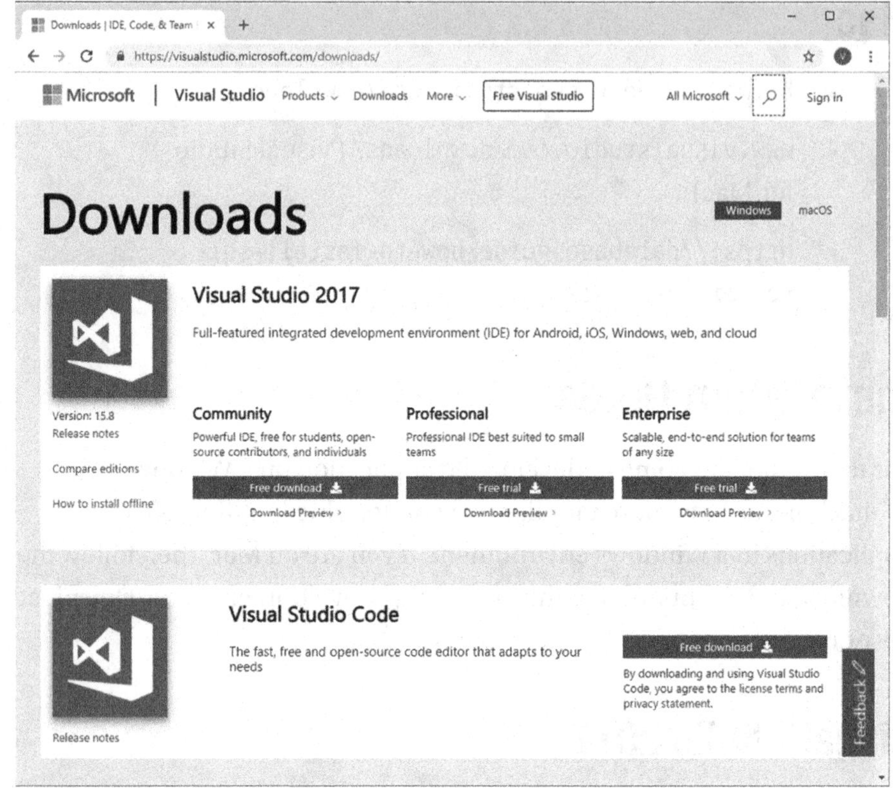

***Figure 1-1.** Visual Studio official download site*

Choose the version that you want to use and click the download button; it should download one of the following Visual Studio installers into your machine's drive:

- **vs_enterprise.exe** for Visual Studio Enterprise
- **vs_professional.exe** for Visual Studio Professional
- **vs_community.exe** for Visual Studio Community

The installer should include everything you need to both install and customize Visual Studio. Now go ahead and double-click the installer that you've downloaded to start kicking the bootstrapper. If you are prompted with a user account control notice, just click **Yes**.

It will then ask you to acknowledge the Microsoft license terms and the Microsoft privacy statement.

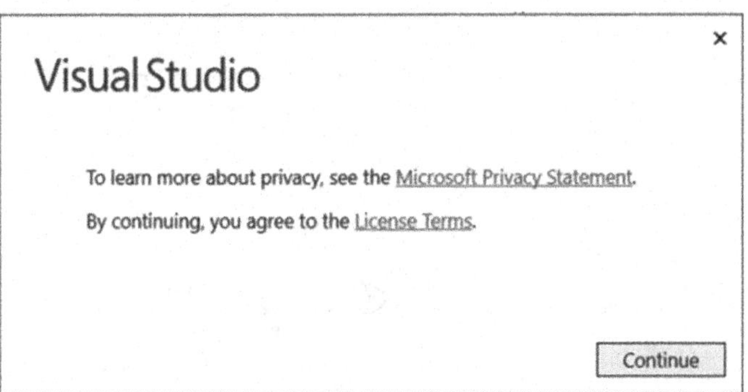

Figure 1-2. *Visual Studio license terms agreement*

Click **Continue** to proceed with the installation.

After the installer is installed, you should be presented with the following view to customize your installation by selecting the feature sets or workloads that you want.

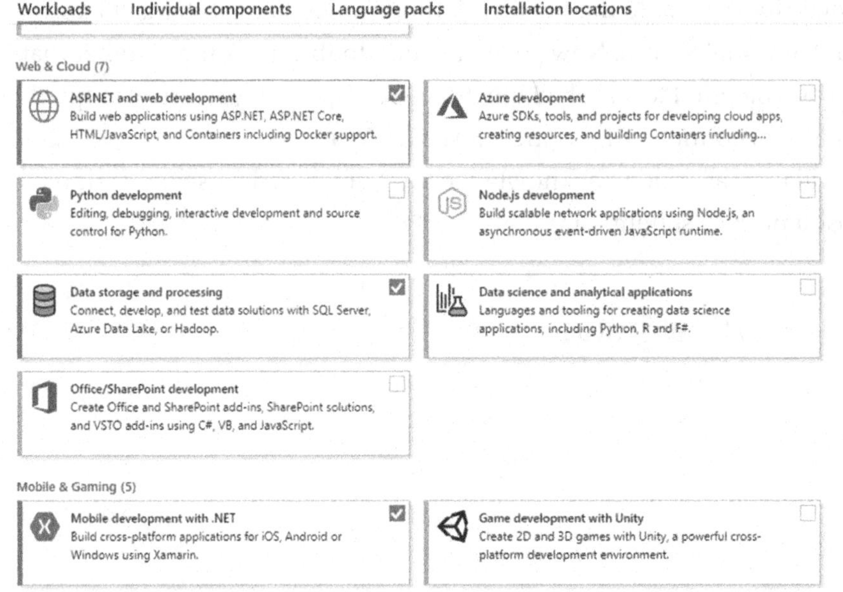

Figure 1-3. *Workload selections*

For building the application in this example, we need to select the following workloads:

- ASP.NET and web development
- Data storage and processing
- Mobile development with .NET

After you select the required workloads, click the **Install** button. A screen should appear showing the status and progress of the installation.

After the new workloads and components are installed, you may click **Launch** to start using Visual Studio.

SQL Server 2017

Microsoft SQL Server is a relational database management system developed by Microsoft. As a database server, it is a software product with the primary function of storing and retrieving data as requested by other software applications (desktop, service, mobile, or web), which may run on either the same or another computer across a network or the Internet.

For simplicity, I'm just going to use the Expression edition of SQL Server 2017 because we will just be creating a basic database with simple tables and storing only a minimal amount of data.

Go ahead and download the SQL Server Express edition at this link: `www.microsoft.com/en-us/sql-server/sql-server-editions-express`. You should be presented with the following page:

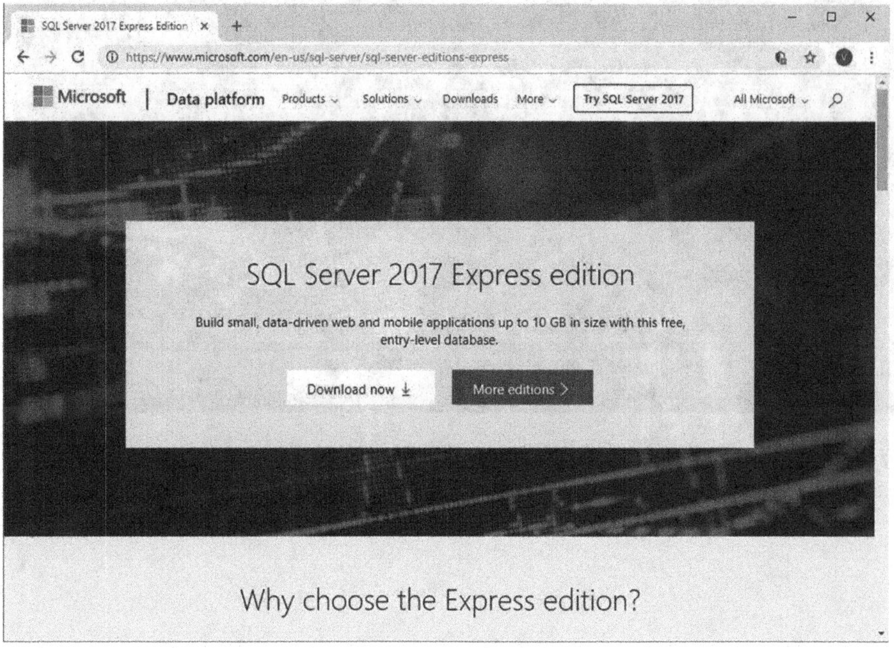

Figure 1-4. *SQL Server official download site*

Click the **Download now** button, and it should download the following SQL Server 2017 Express installer into your machine drive:

- SQLServer2017-SSEI-Expr.exe

Run the SQLServer2017-SSEI-Expr.exe installer, and it should show a screen that looks like this:

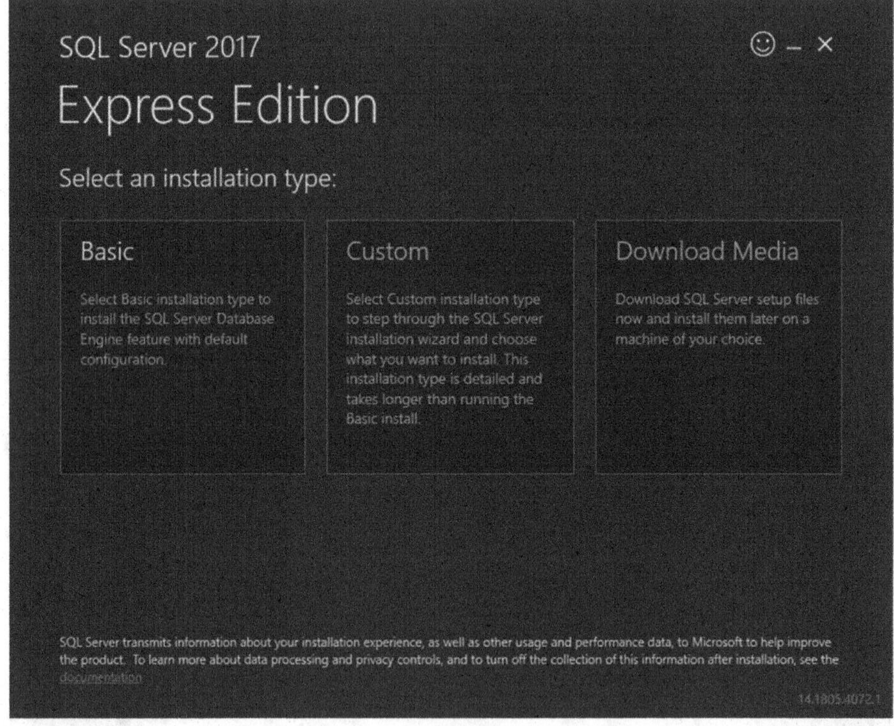

Figure 1-5. *SQL Server installation selection*

Just select the **Basic** installation type, and it should take you to the following screen and ask you to accept the Microsoft SQL Server license terms:

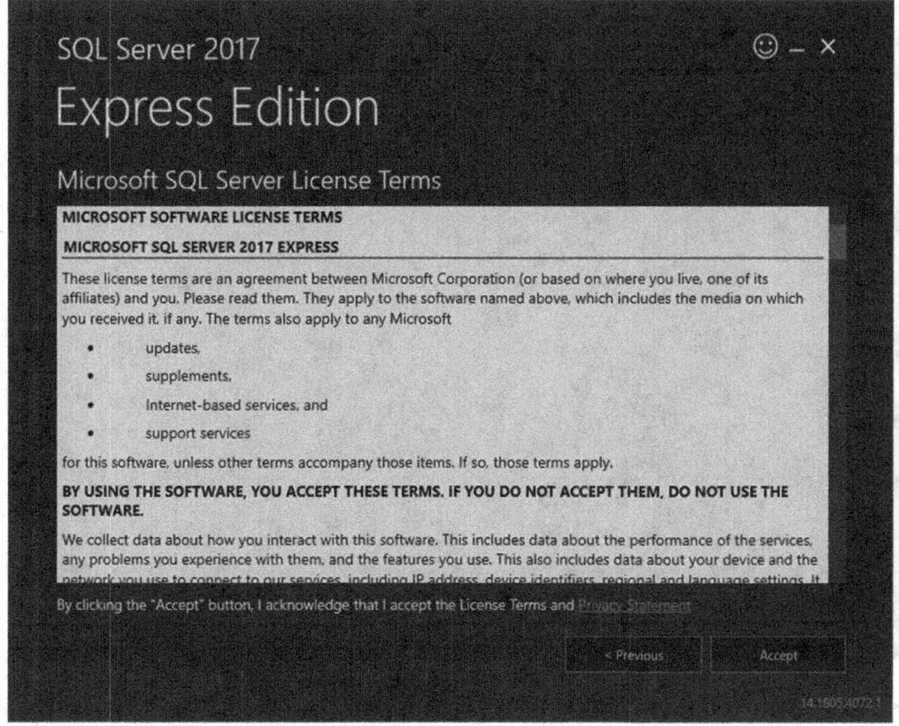

Figure 1-6. *SQL Server license terms agreement*

Click **Accept**. It should now take you to the following screen:

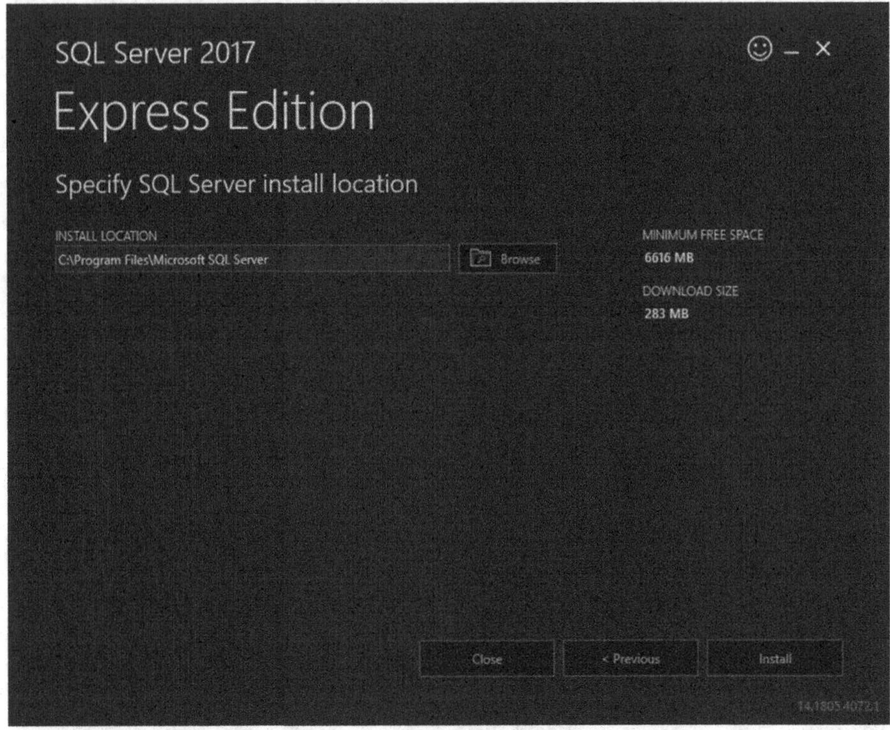

Figure 1-7. *SQL Server specify install location*

Select the target location for installing the SQL Server. If you are satisfied with the default install location or your current selected install location, then go ahead and click **Install**.

The next screen should display the installation status and progress just like in the following figure:

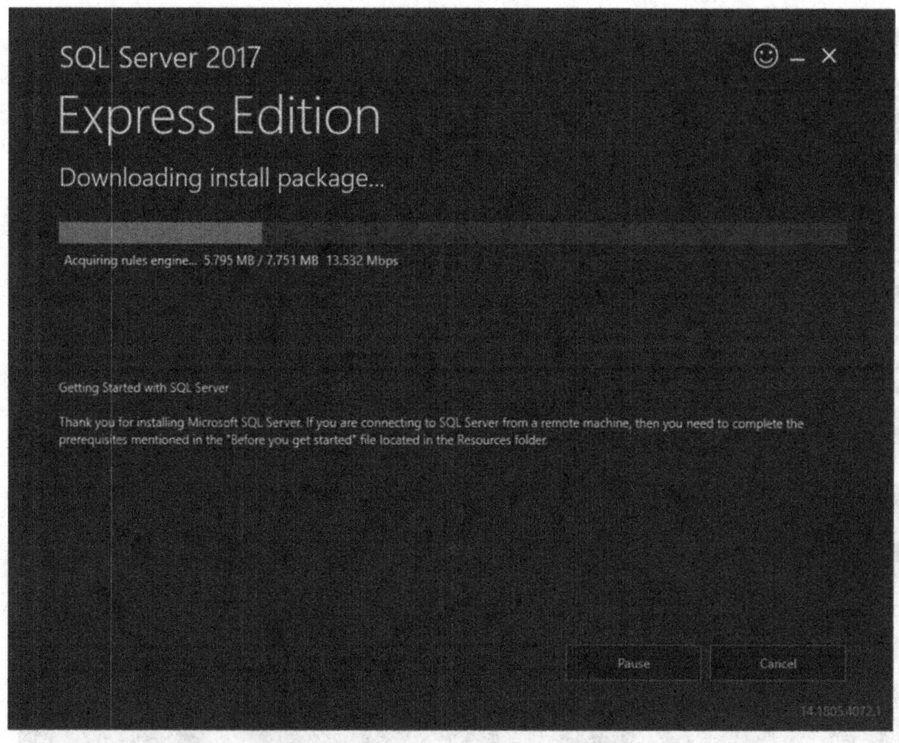

Figure 1-8. *SQL Server installation progress*

You may need to wait a few minutes to complete the installation. Once the installation is done, you should be presented with the following screen:

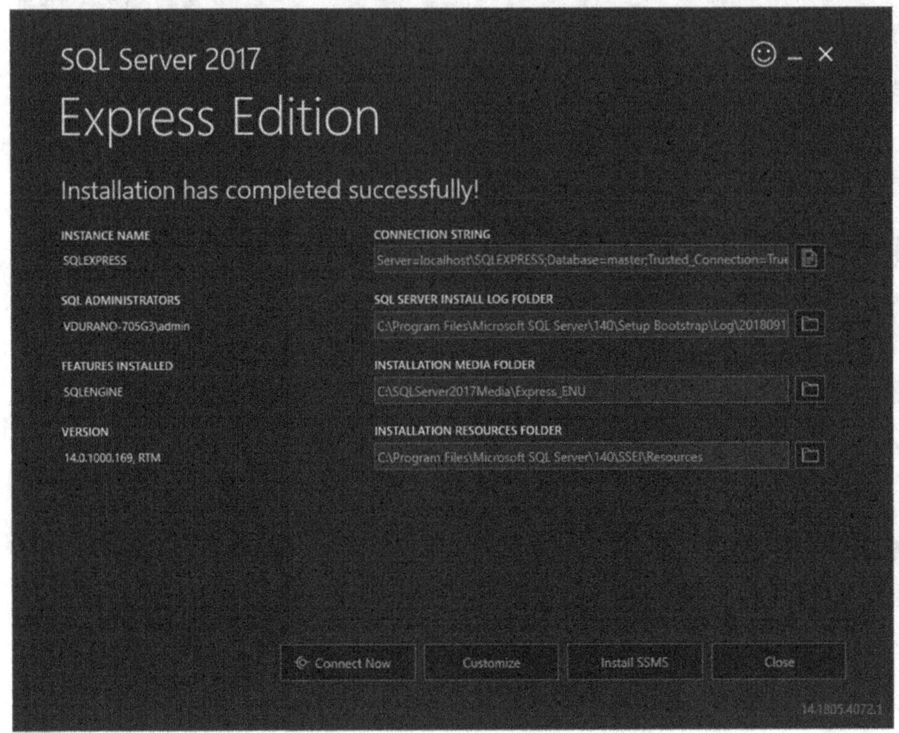

Figure 1-9. *SQL Server installation summary*

The final installation screen shows the summary of the installation. It also allows you to open the SQL Server directly and customize the installation. The next step is to install SSMS. Click the **Install SSMS** button and it should take you to a download link. The latest version as of the time of writing is SSMS 9.7.

Run the online installer after you have downloaded the SSMS from the Microsoft download site. You should be presented with the following screen:

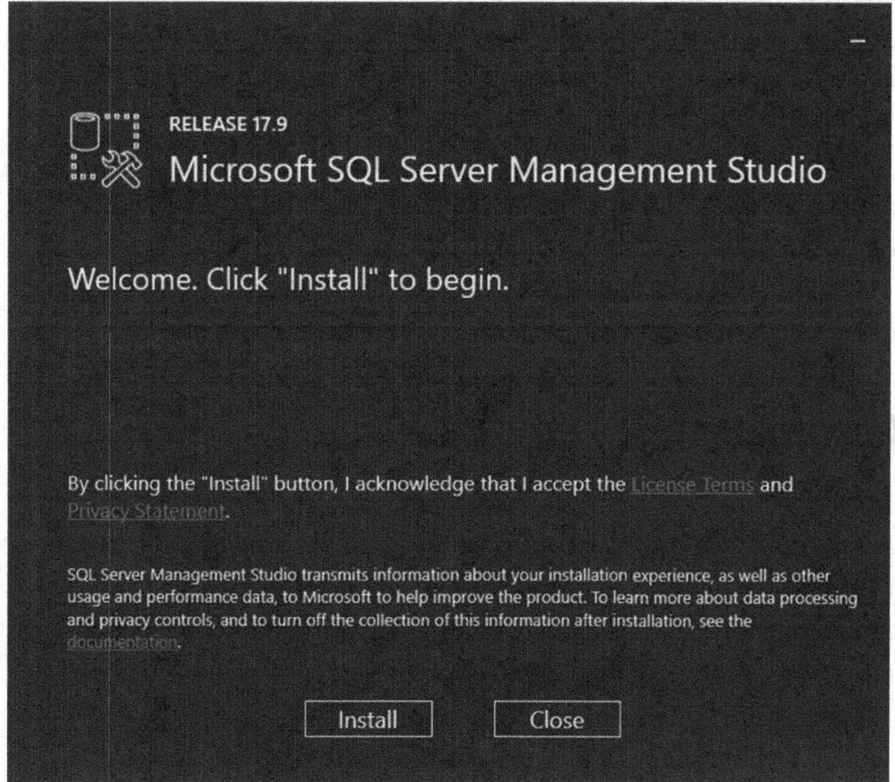

Figure 1-10. *SSMS installation*

Click **Install**. After the setup is complete, just click **Close**.

We will use SSMS to query, design, and manage the database later in the Chapter 3.

Five Players, One Goal

As you can see from the “Prerequisites” section, we are going to use various technologies to build this whole game application to fulfill a goal. At this point, you should already have the needed frameworks installed in your machine as long as you properly installed the required workloads mentioned in the “Installation Guide” section.

Our main goal is to build a simple data-driven Working Memory game application using cutting-edge technologies: Xamarin.Forms, ASP.NET Web API, EF, ASP.NET MVC, and ASP.NET SignalR.

Before we discuss the high-level process flow for how each technology connects together, let’s take a look at a brief overview of them.

Xamarin.Forms

Building mobile applications that target multiple platforms such as Android, iOS, and UWP has always been a time-consuming pain, as you have to deal with different programming languages and platform-specific implementation. Aside from that, maintaining multiple code repositories to do essentially the same thing is tedious at best, and at worst can become a nightmare.

As a .NET developer who knows C#, Xamarin will provide you with the functionality you need. It promises to deliver mobile apps with a shared code base; however, that shared code base is on the application logic side of things. Traditional Xamarin.iOS, Xamarin.Android, and Xamarin.UWP development still requires that the UIs be written separately from each other, and that is no small task.

Xamarin.Forms offers a significant time savings in this regard. Its claim to fame is that it abstracts the UI of each platform—the individual operating system controls and navigation metaphors—into a common layer that can be used to build applications for iOS, Android, and UWP with both a shared application layer and a UI layer.

Xamarin.Forms is a mobile application framework for generating cross-platform UIs, and it couples that with .NET Standard to share code, making it an even more favorable choice. Here's the definition taken from the official documentation: `https://docs.microsoft.com/en-us/xamarin/xamarin-forms/`

> *Xamarin.Forms exposes a complete cross-platform UI toolkit for .NET developers. Build fully native Android, iOS, and Universal Windows Platform apps using C# in Visual Studio.*

Xamarin.Forms offers so much more in addition to 20+ cross-platform UI controls that work across platforms.

Xamarin vs. Xamarin.Forms

Xamarin (sometimes called Xamarin Native), enables developers to create fully rich iOS, Android, macOS, watchOS, tvOS, and Windows applications in C# and Visual Studio with 100% API coverage of each platform in C#. You develop the UI natively for each platform, but share all your business logic, which on average is 60–80% of your application. This approach gives you 100% API access, 100% of the UI, and of course the best performance.

Xamarin.Forms offers up a cross-platform UI that is based on XAML or C# and sits on top of Xamarin Native itself. This works across iOS, Android, UWP, macOS, and others supported by the community. The language is similar, as it is XAML, but not identical, as the controls and names are a bit different. However, picking it up is easy, and Xamarin and Microsoft have great documentation on it.

ASP.NET Web API

The ASP.NET Web API is an extensible framework for building HTTP-based services that can be accessed in different applications on different platforms. It works more or less the same way as the ASP.NET MVC web application, except that it sends data as a response instead of

HTML View. It is like a web service or WCF (Windows Communication Foundation) service, but the exception is that it only supports HTTP protocol. Here's the definition taken from the official documentation: `https://msdn.microsoft.com/en-us/library/hh833994(v=vs.108).aspx`

> *ASP.NET Web API is a framework that makes it easy to build HTTP services that reach a broad range of clients, including browsers and mobile devices. ASP.NET Web API is an ideal platform for building RESTful applications on the .NET Framework.*

EF

EF is a tried and tested object-relational mapper (ORM) for .NET with many years of feature development and stabilization.

According to the official documentation: `https://docs.microsoft.com/en-us/ef/ef6/`

> *As an O/RM, EF reduces the impedance mismatch between the relational and object-oriented worlds, enabling developers to write applications that interact with data stored in relational databases using strongly-typed .NET objects that represent the application's domain, and eliminating the need for a large portion of the data access "plumbing" code that they usually need to write.*

If you are still confused about what an ORM does and how EF functions in the application, don't worry, as we will see details about it in the Chapter 3.

ASP.NET MVC

The ASP.NET MVC is a web application framework developed by Microsoft, which implements the MVC pattern. Here's the definition taken from the official documentation: `https://msdn.microsoft.com/en-us/library/dd381412(v=vs.108).aspx`

> *The Model-View-Controller (MVC) architectural pattern separates an application into three main components: the model, the view, and the controller. The ASP.NET MVC framework provides an alternative to the ASP.NET Web Forms pattern for creating Web applications. The ASP.NET MVC framework is a lightweight, highly testable presentation framework that (as with Web Forms-based applications) is integrated with existing ASP.NET features, such as master pages and membership-based authentication. The MVC framework is defined in the System.Web.Mvc assembly.*

ASP.NET SignalR

ASP.NET SignalR is typically used to add any kind of "real-time" web functionality to your ASP.NET application. While chat is often used as an example, you can do a whole lot more. Any time a user refreshes a web page to see new data, or the page implements long polling to retrieve new data, it is a candidate for using SignalR. Examples include dashboards and monitoring applications, collaborative applications (such as simultaneous editing of documents), job progress updates, and real-time forms.

Here's the definition taken from the official documentation: https://docs.microsoft.com/en-us/aspnet/signalr/overview/getting-started/introduction-to-signalr

> *ASP.NET SignalR is a library for ASP.NET developers that simplifies the process of adding real-time web functionality to applications. Real-time web functionality is the ability to have server code push content to connected clients instantly as it becomes available, rather than having the server wait for a client to request new data.*

Wrap-Up

Now that you know the basic overview of each technology and framework that we will be using to build the applications, it's time for us to take a moment and see how to connect the dots in the picture. The following diagram illustrates the high-level process by which the technologies connect to each other.

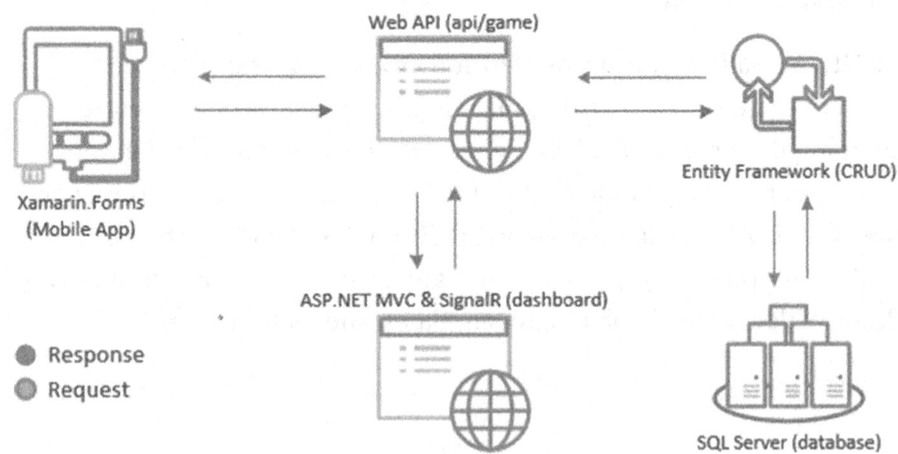

***Figure 1-11.** High-level diagram of how the technologies interact*

Based on the preceding illustration, we are going to need to build the following applications:

- A mobile app that targets both iOS and Android platform
- A Web API app that exposes some public-facing API endpoints
- A web app that hosts a real-time dashboard
- A database that stores and persists data

Since this demo is primarily focusing on the game development, then the process flow will start at the mobile app. A mobile app requests data for storing and retrieving a user's information via a REST API call (ASP.NET Web API). All requests will then be handled by the Web API server. The Web API server acts as the central gateway to access a resource from a database; it serves the request made and returns a response when necessary. The Web API server does not hold the actual data but contains the actual implementation of how the data is being retrieved or stored and handles the CRUD operations using EF. All data changes made by EF will be executed and reflected against the SQL Server database. The SQL Server database serves as a medium of storage to hold and persist data.

The beauty of the REST service is that it allows different client applications (e.g., desktop, mobile, web, or services) to consume API via endpoints for as long as it supports HTTP protocols. Based on the preceding illustration, a web app can also request data to the Web API server. The web app serves as the dashboard page for displaying the information in real time using ASP.NET SignalR.

To summarize, we are going to build a mobile application using **(1) Xamarin.Forms** that can target both iOS and Android platforms. The mobile app is where the actual game is implemented, and also where users will be allowed to register. We will build an **(2) ASP.NET Web API** server application to handle CRUD operations using **(3) EF**. The Web API project will serve as the central gateway to handle data requests that come from the mobile app and the web app. We will also build a web application to display the real-time dashboard for displaying player ranking using **(4) ASP.NET MVC** and **(5) ASP.NET SignalR**. Finally, we are going to create a database for storing players' information and scores in SQL Server.

CHAPTER 2

Getting Started

Before we get our hands dirty with actual coding, let's try to understand the application process flow first so that you can have a better picture about the whole flow of the application from the user's perspective.

Application Flow

The application that we are going to build has three main layers:

- Mobile application
- Web API Server
- Web application

The following diagram shows the application process flow of each layer and how the layers interact to achieve a goal:

V. M. S. Durano, *Understanding Game Application Development*,
https://doi.org/10.1007/978-1-4842-4264-3_2

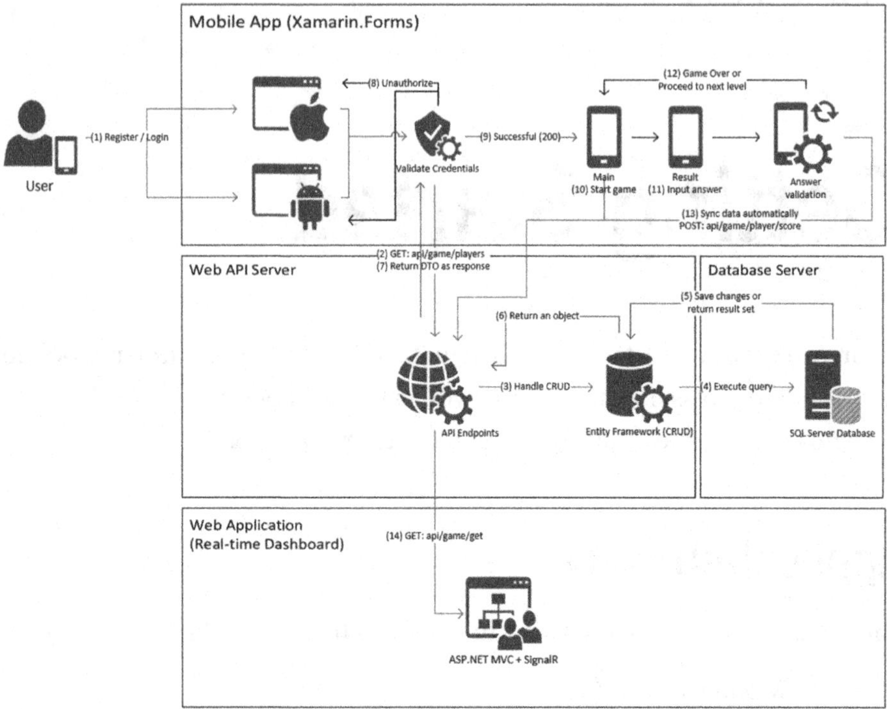

Figure 2-1. *Application process flow*

Mobile Application Process Flow

Let's start with the first layer, the **mobile app**. In order for a user to start playing the game, they need to register an account first. During registration, a user will simply need to provide their e-mail address, first name, last name, and that's it. I've chosen not to include a password upon registration for the sake of simplicity and to remove the complexity of managing user accounts. With that being said, the mobile application will simply ask for the user's e-mail address to log in to the system. If you look at the preceding diagram, the mobile application talks to the Web API server to get the user information by issuing an HTTP Get request before validating the credentials. The Web API Server handles the request from the mobile app and returns a JSON response back to the mobile app. Keep in mind that the mobile application also stores the user information locally. This is to ensure that the system has a local copy of data when a user plays the game offline.

Now when a user's credentials are successfully validated, the user will be navigated to the main screen of the application, wherein they can start playing the game. Otherwise, a validation error that the credentials are invalid or do not exist is prompted.

During the game, the application will randomly beep a sound, blink an image, or vibrate the device within a given amount of time in seconds. When the time has elapsed, the application will automatically take the user to the next screen, where they can input their answers. After they submit the answers, the system will validate this input and either display a "congratulations" message and allow them to proceed to the next level or display a "game over" message if their answers are incorrect. The system will also automatically sync the user's highest score and level after the system has validated the answers.

What's exciting about this game is that the more you move to a next level, the faster it triggers the different event types until you can't remember which type of event occurs.

Web API Server Process Flow

As a recap, the API server acts as a central gateway for handling HTTP requests from a client application. In this particular setup, the API server handles both mobile and web app requests and then delegates the request into the data access sublayer using EF to process the data. An HTTP request can be a form of Insert, Update, Read, or Delete.

The EF manipulates the data through a strongly typed .NET object and then translates that into a SQL query command and executes it to reflect and persist the changes in the data to the SQL Server database.

Web Application Process Flow

The web app is nothing but a page that displays the user ranking dashboard (a.k.a. leaderboard). This page is an ASP.NET MVC application that asynchronously listens to a data change by subscribing to a Web API endpoint and then displays the changes in real time using ASP.NET SignalR. Real-time changes occur when a manual sync or automatic sync is triggered from the mobile app.

Game Overview

This section discusses the game mechanics and objective.

Mechanics

During the game and as soon as you hit the **Start** button, the application will randomly play different event types within a given time interval expressed in milliseconds. The trigger cycle has a time interval also expressed in milliseconds. For example, within 10 seconds, the app randomly plays different event types such as blinking an image, playing a sound, or activating vibration on the device in a 2-second cycle. At the succeeding levels, the 2-second cycle interval will decrease, which causes the events to trigger much faster than at the previous level.

To make it clearer, the following diagram shows how the game flows:

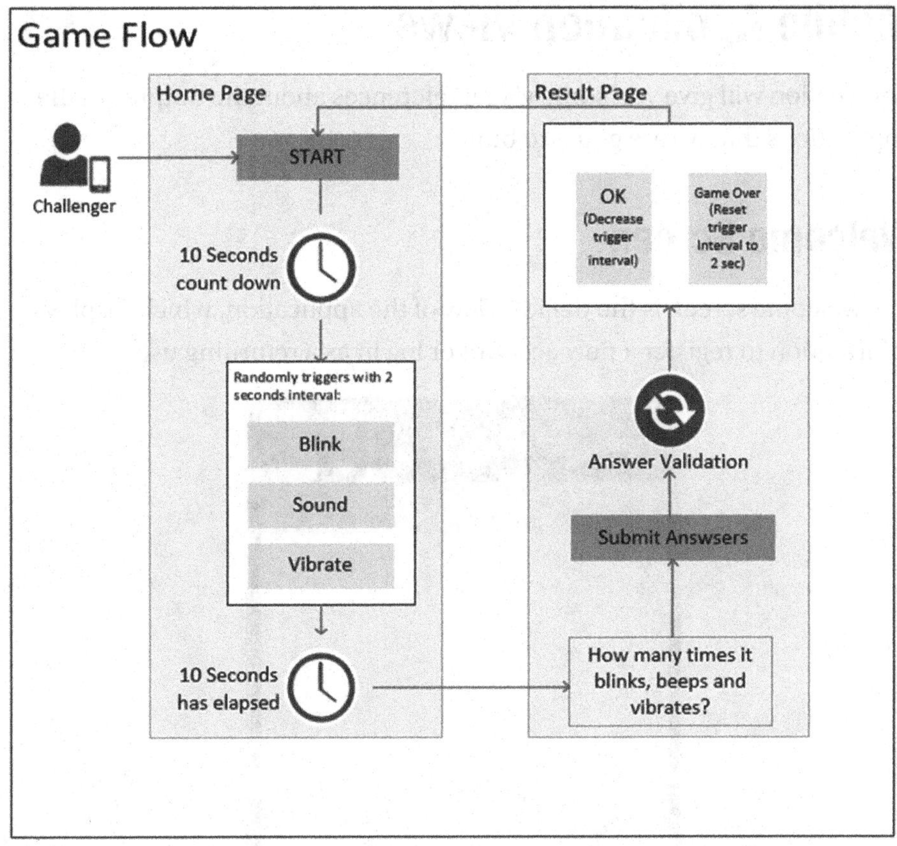

Figure 2-2. Game flow

Objective

The objective of this game is very simple; you just need to count and memorize how many times the light blinks on, the speaker beeps, and the device vibrates within a span of time. The higher your level is, the faster it blinks, beeps, and vibrates. This will test how great your memory is.

Mobile Application Views

This section will give you some visual references about the outputs of the applications that we are going to build.

Welcome Screen

The welcome screen is the default view of the application, which displays information to register a new account or log in as a returning user.

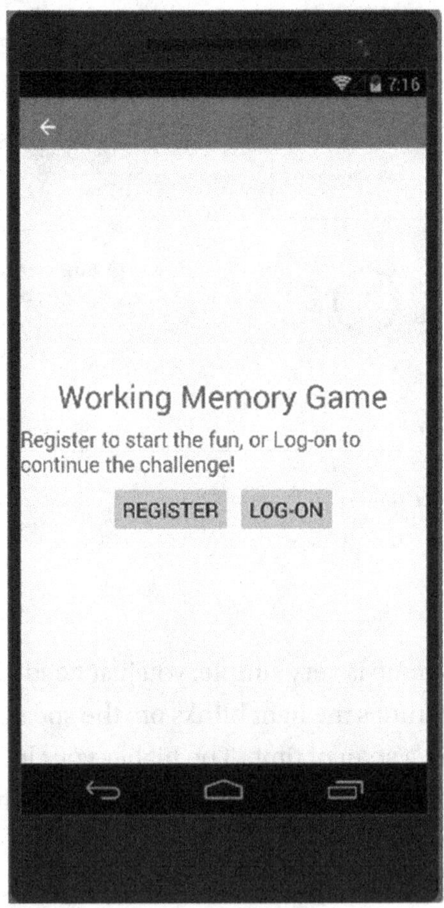

Figure 2-3. *Mobile app welcome view*

Registration Screen

Clicking the **REGISTER** button will display the registration screen, which allows users to register using first name, last name, and e-mail. The **LOG-ON** button will display the login screen, which allows a returning user to enter their registered e-mail.

Here's a running view of the registration screen:

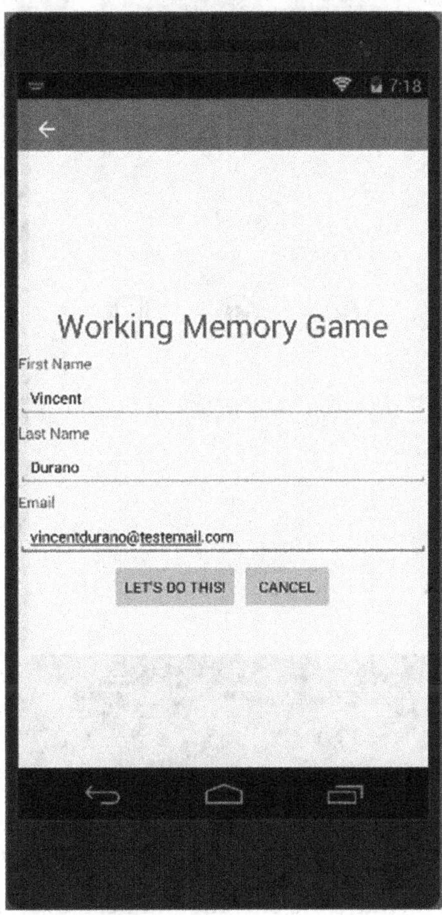

***Figure 2-4.** Mobile app register view*

Main Screen

Once the user has successfully been registered or logged on to the system, they will be redirected to the main screen, as shown in the following figure.

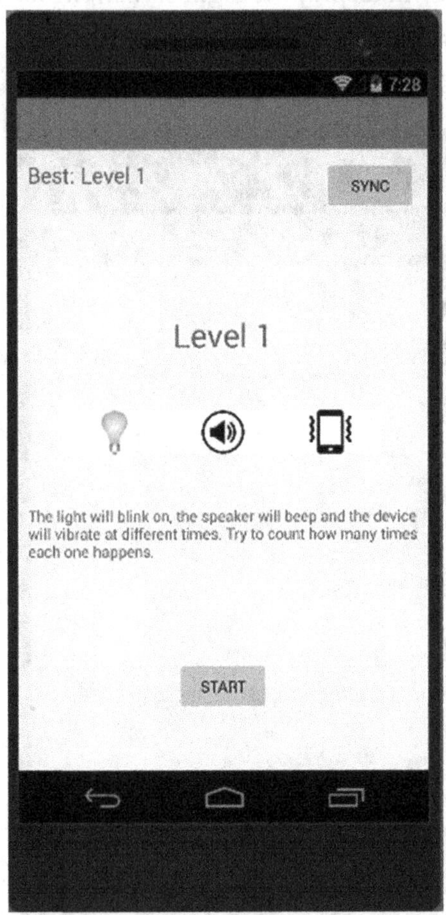

***Figure 2-5.** Mobile app home view*

The main screen displays the current and best level scores and as well as a **SYNC** button to allow users to manually sync their scores in the database. It also displays three main images: a bulb, a speaker, and a device that indicates a vibration.

Clicking the **START** button will start the game within a short period of time and turn the button text to **GAME STARTED...,** as shown in the following figure.

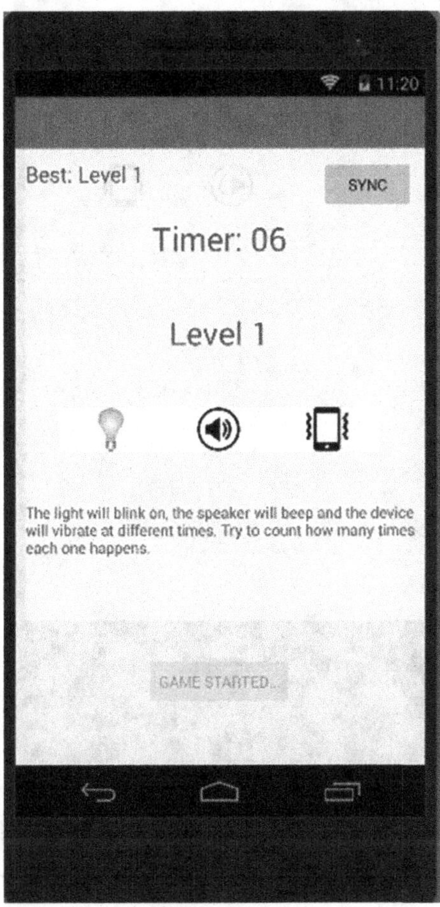

***Figure 2-6.** Mobile app game view*

Result Screen

After the time has elapsed, it will bring users to the result screen, wherein they can input their answers for how many times each event happened.

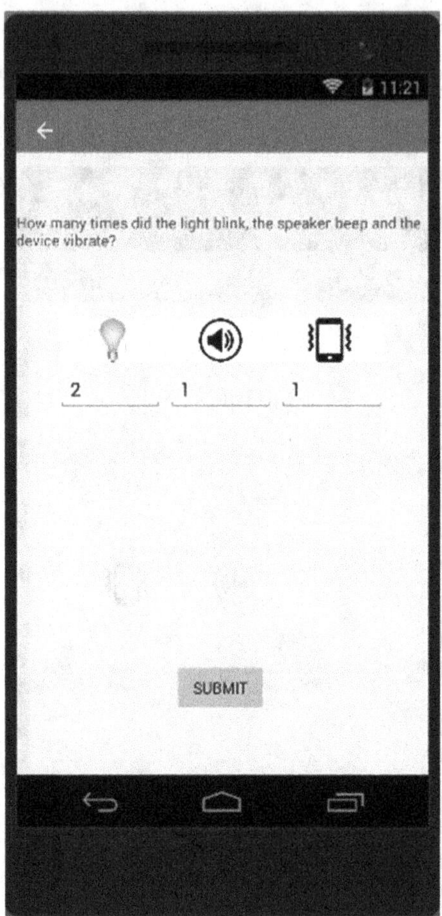

***Figure 2-7.** Mobile app answer view*

Clicking the **SUBMIT** button will trigger the system to validate the answers and determines whether the user gave them correctly and thus may proceed to the next level or whether the game should be restarted at the current level. Note that the score will be automatically synced to the database once the user surpasses their current best score.

Here are some screenshots of the results:

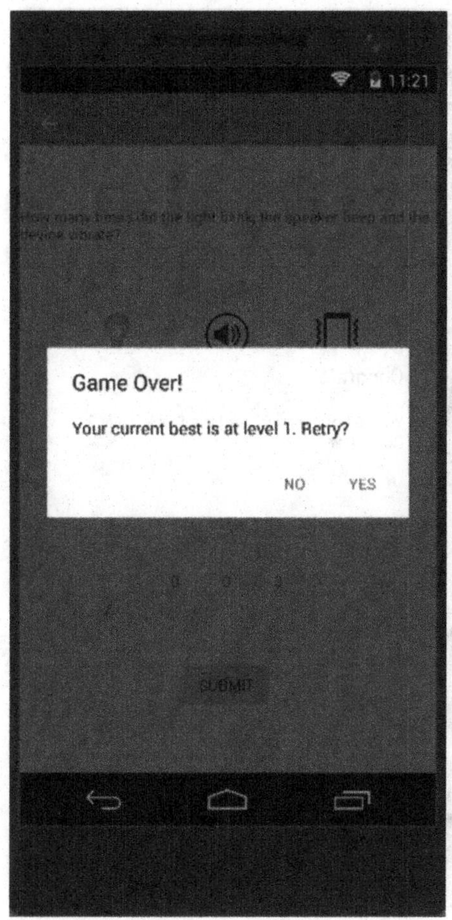

***Figure 2-8.** Mobile app results view: Game Over!*

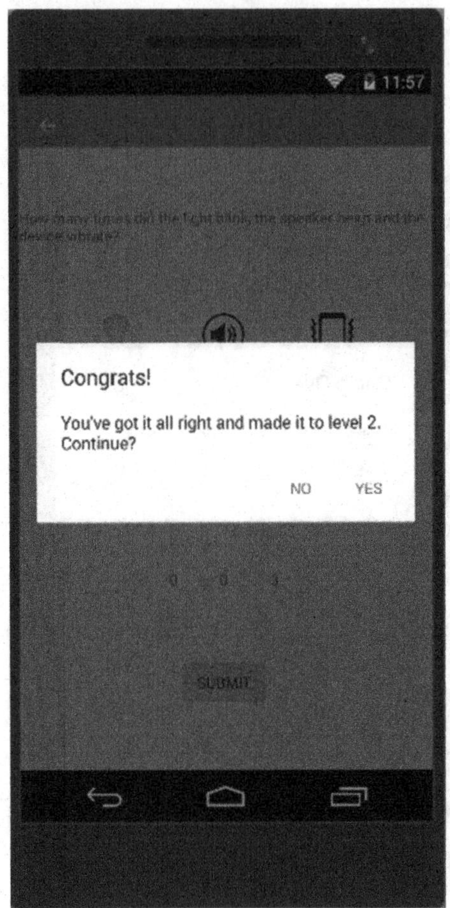

Figure 2-9. *Mobile app results view: Congrats!*

Web Application View

Here's the sample output of the real-time leaderboard page built using ASP.NET MVC and ASP.NET SignalR.

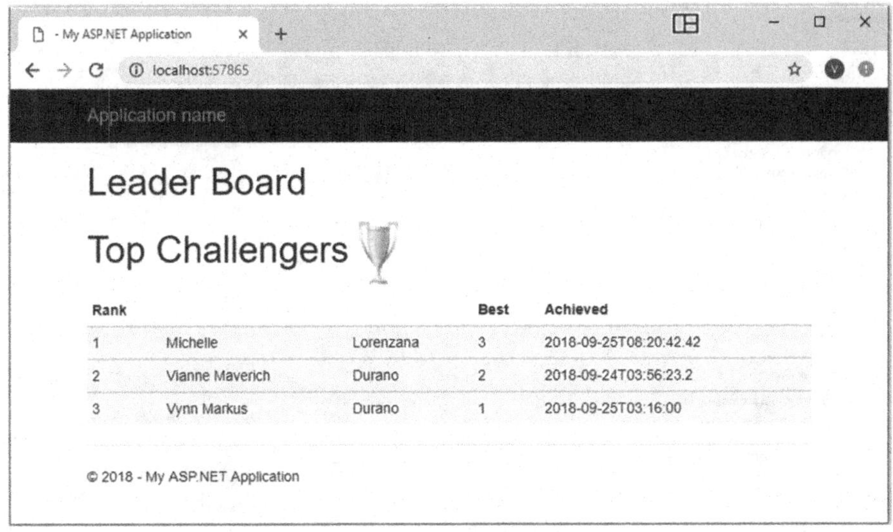

Figure 2-10. *Web app real-time ranking view*

That's it. Now that you have some visual reference for what the app will look like, it's time for us to build the applications and get our hands dirty with real code examples.

Creating the Core Projects for Mobile App

I'll try to keep this demo as simple as possible, so beginners can easily follow. By "simple," I mean that I will limit the discussion of theories and concepts, but instead jump directly into the mud and let us get our hands dirty with code examples.

Let's go ahead and launch Visual Studio 2017 and then create a new blank XAML app (Xamarin.Forms) by going through **File ➤ New ➤ Project**. You should be presented with a **New Project** window dialog. In the left pane of the dialog under the **Installed** item, drill down to **Visual C# ➤ Cross-Platform** and then select **Mobile App (Xamarin.Forms)** just like in the following figure.

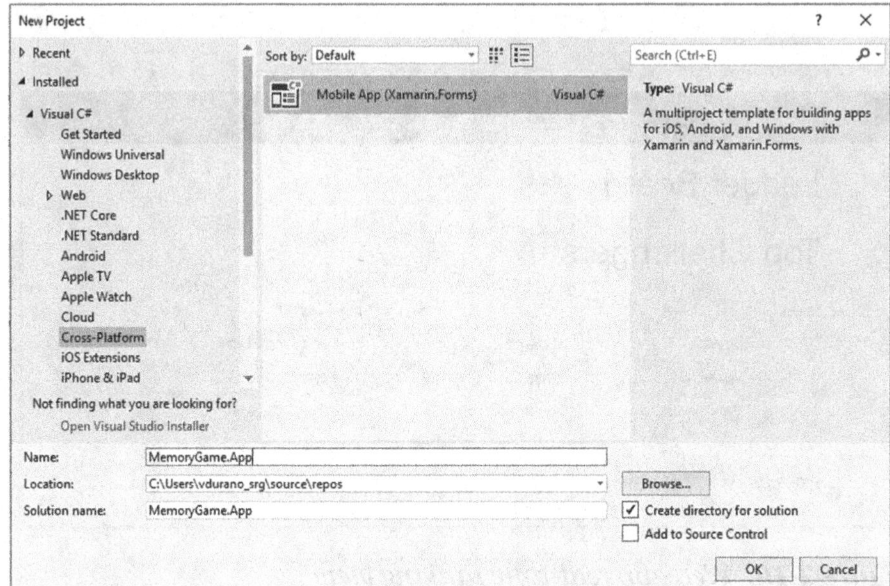

Figure 2-11. *Create new Xamarin.Forms project*

Although you can freely name the project to your preference, for this demo let's just name it **MemoryGame.App,** as it suits well to what we are going to build. Click **OK** and it should bring up the following window dialog.

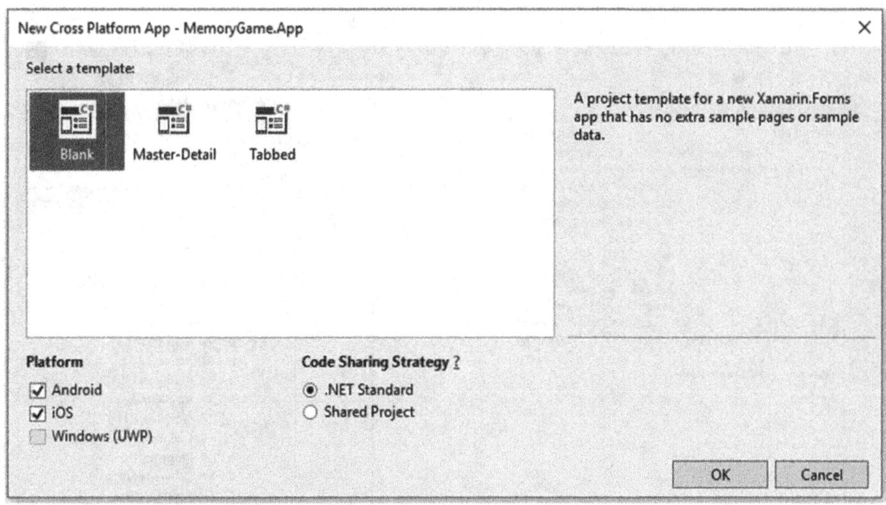

Figure 2-12. *Blank template*

Select the **Blank** template, and under Platform, tick the **Android** and **iOS** options. Select **.NET Standard** as Code Sharing Strategy, and then click **OK** to let Visual Studio generate the necessary files for you.

It may take a moment to generate the files and dependencies depending on your machine and Internet speed.

After Visual Studio is done generating the default files for the project and pulling the necessary dependencies, it should show something like the following.

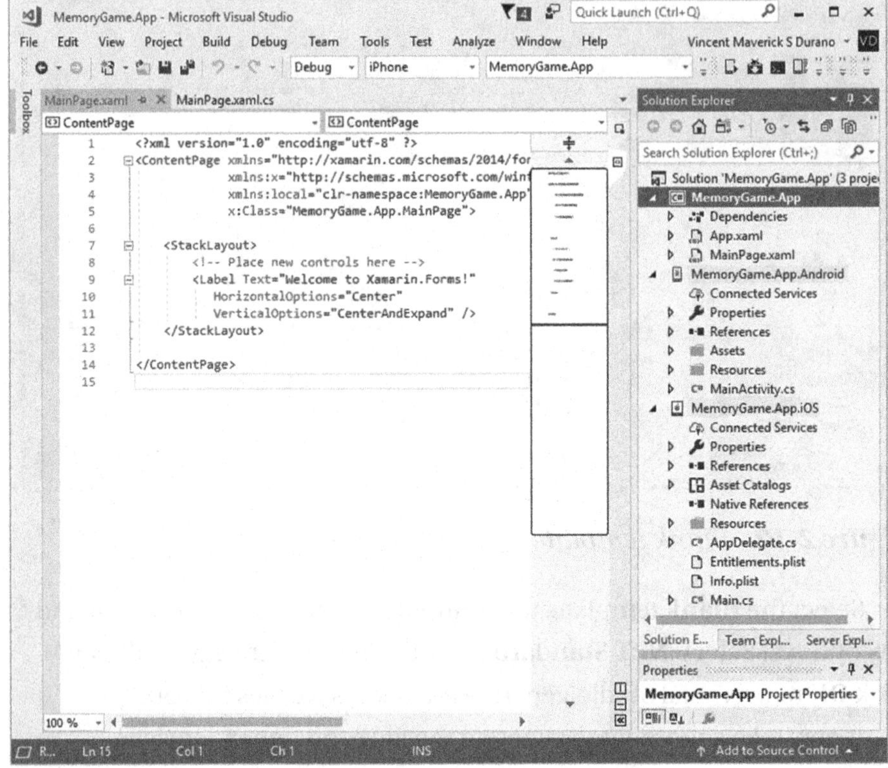

Figure 2-13. Default generated files

The Xamarin.Forms project template basically generates the following three main projects:

- MemoryGame.App
- MemoryGame.App.Android
- MemoryGame.App.iOS

Note That the solution only contains the .Android and .iOS projects. We omitted the .UWP project, and so we will be focusing on Android and iOS apps instead.

Overview and Anatomy

Let's take a quick overview of each project generated.

MemoryGame.App

In 2011, Microsoft released a new type of class libraries called Portable Class Libraries (PCLs). A PCL is a project type that creates a binary file compatible with multiple frameworks. The previous version of Xamarin. Forms uses PCL to enable you to choose a combination of platforms that you want your code to run on. PCLs enable centralized code sharing, which allows developers to write and test code in a single project that can be consumed by other libraries or applications.

However, the available APIs are reduced each time a new target framework is selected. For example, if a class is available in .NET Framework 4.5.1 but not in Windows Universal 10.0, it won't be available in the PCL targeting both these frameworks. The combinations of the target frameworks are called profiles.

While PCLs were a breakthrough at the time of their creation, it was sometimes difficult to find information on which APIs were available and where to find them. In time, it became clear to the .NET team that a simpler approach was needed, and that's where .NET Standard fits.

The MemoryGame.App is a .NET Standard Library project. The prerelease version of the Xamarin.Forms 2.3.5 added compatibility with .NET Standard.

.NET Standard is a formal specification of .NET APIs that is intended to be available on all .NET runtimes (such as .NET Framework, Mono, and .NET Core). In real terms, you can think of this as a simplified yet expanded PCL. Any code added to a .NET Standard library can be used on any runtime that supports the .NET Standard platform. In addition, we get expanded access to APIs within the .NET base class libraries, and this supports more platforms. For more information, see `https://blogs.msdn.microsoft.com/dotnet/2016/09/26/introducing-net-standard/`.

Here's the anatomy of the Xamarin.Forms .NET Standard project:

Folder/File	Purpose
Dependencies	Contains both NuGet and SDK dependencies for the project.
App.xaml	Responsible for instantiating the first page that will be displayed by the application on each platform.
MainPage.xaml	Initializes the main page components.

MemoryGame.App.Android

The MemoryGame.App.Android contains Android-specific configuration and files needed to run the application. Here's the anatomy of the Android project:

Folder/File	Purpose
Connected Services	Allows service providers to create Visual Studio extensions that can be added to a project without leaving the IDE. It also allows you to connect your ASP.NET core application or mobile services to Azure storage services. Connected Services takes care of all the references and connection code, and modifies your configuration files accordingly.
Properties	Contains the AndroidManifest.xml file, which describes all the requirements for our Xamarin.Android application, including name, version number, and permissions. It also contains the AssemblyInfo.cs file, in which you can define assembly details such as title, description, copyright info, version, and more.

Folder/File	Purpose
References	Contains the assemblies required to build and run the application.
Assets	Contains the files the application needs to run, including fonts, local data files, and text files.
Resources	Contains application resources such as strings, images, and layouts. You can access these resources in code through the generated resource class.
MainActivity.cs	A C# class that contains code for initializing and loading the application.

MemoryGame.App.iOS

The MemoryGame.App.iOS contains iOS-specific configurations and files needed to run the application. Here's the anatomy of the iOS project:

Folder/File	Purpose
Asset Catalogs	Just like the Assets folder in the .Android project, this contains the files the application needs to run, including fonts, local data files, and text files.
Native References	This is where you add assemblies specific to the iOS platform.
Resources	Contains application resources such as strings, images, and layouts. You can access these resources in code through the generated resource class.
AppDelegate.cs	This class is responsible for launching the UI of the application, as well as listening (and optionally responding) to application events from iOS.

(continued)

Folder/File	Purpose
Entitlements.plist	Used to specify entitlements and to sign the application bundle. In essence, Entitlements are special app capabilities and security permissions granted to applications that are correctly configured to use them.
Info.plist	Contains metadata to the system. This file typically contains the keys and their corresponding values for the application's configuration bundle.
Main.cs	The main entry point of the application.

Architecture Fundamentals

A `Xamarin.Forms` application is architected in the same way as a traditional cross-platform application. Shared code is typically placed in a .NET Standard library, and platform-specific applications consume the shared code. The following diagram shows an overview of this relationship for the `MemoryGame.App` application:

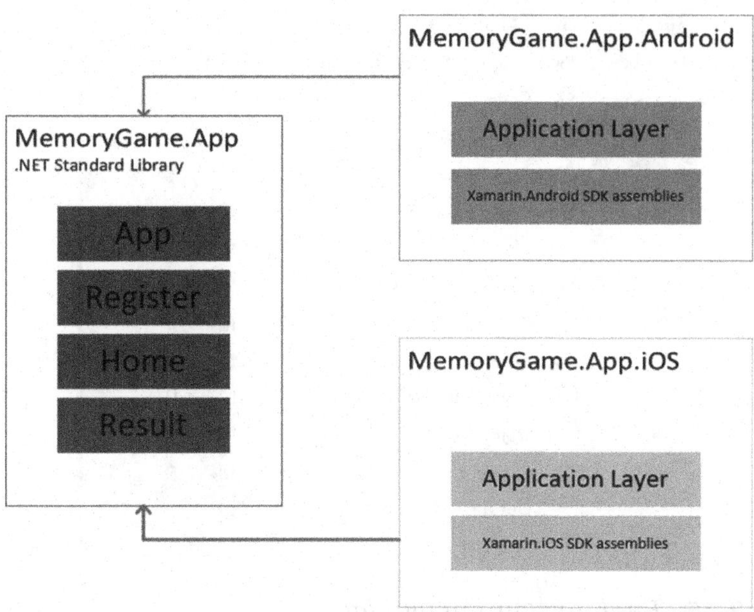

***Figure 2-14.** Xamarin.Forms architecture fundamentals*

First Run

To ensure that we have everything we need for our core mobile application projects, let's try to build and run the project. Let's start by enabling the Output window by going through the Visual Studio main menu under **View ➤ Output** just like in the following figure:

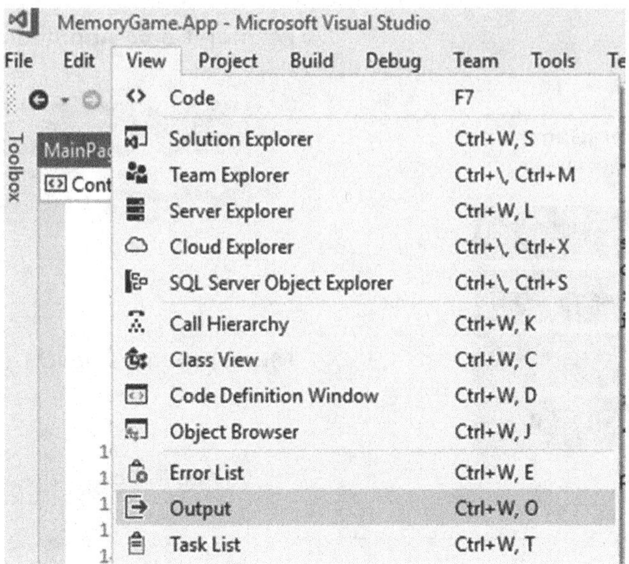

Figure 2-15. *Enabling Output window*

Next, let's try building the whole projects by right-clicking the Solution level then selecting **Build Solution,** as shown in the following figure:

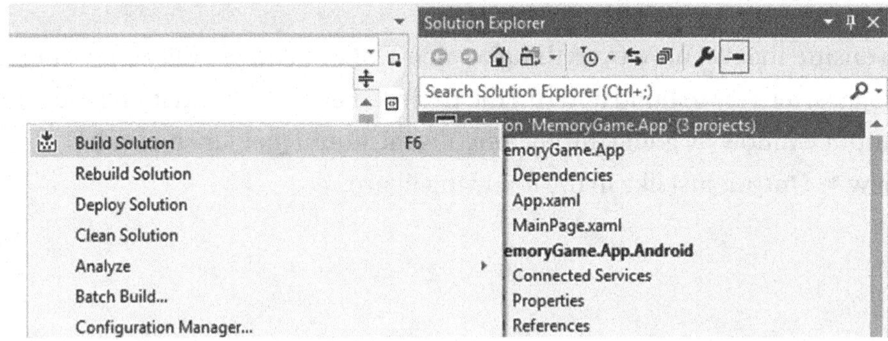

Figure 2-16. *Building the project's solution*

Or, you could simply hit the **F6** key.

The **Output** window should show the build results. If everything goes well and builds successfully, then we can start running the apps. The good thing is that the Visual Studio Emulator for Android is included when you install Visual Studio 2017 to develop Xamarin apps. This means that you can test and run the application right away without needing to download and install the Android emulator separately.

If you don't want to use the default emulator that comes with the Visual Studio 2017, then you can also download an emulator separately.

- Windows 8.1 and Windows 10: `https://visualstudio.microsoft.com/vs/msft-android-emulator/`
- Windows 7: You can use Android SDK/Google or use a third-party emulator such as GenyMotion/Xamarin Android Player.

For this demo, I will just use the default emulator in Visual Studio 2017.

Xamarin.Android

Let's try to run the Xamarin.Android project first. To do that, we need to set the Xamarin.Android project as the startup project by right-clicking the MemoryGame.App.Android and then select **Set as StartUp Project**.

The **MemoryGame.App.Android** project should be highlighted from the Solution. Now click the **Play** button to run the project in the Android emulator as shown in the following figure:

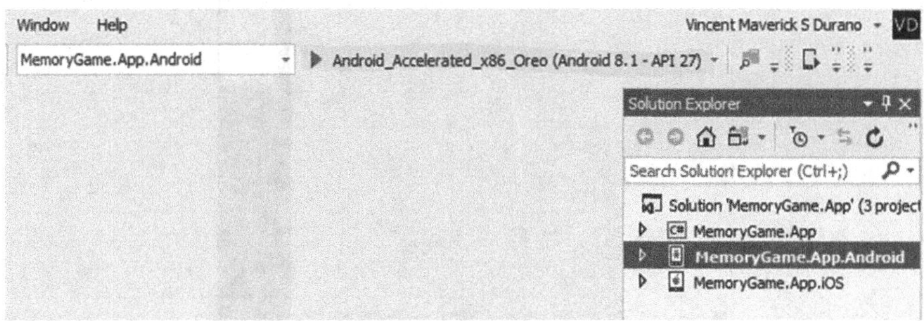

Figure 2-17. *Running the Xamarin.Android project for the first time*

Note If you are prompted with a performance warning that says the emulator will run unaccelerated, just click the "Start Anyway" button to launch the emulator.

After the emulator starts, Visual Studio will build the application then Xamarin.Android will deploy the app to the emulator. The emulator runs the app with the configured virtual device image. An example of the Android emulator is displayed in the following screenshot. In this example, the emulator is running the application with the default page that says "Welcome to Xamarin.Forms!"

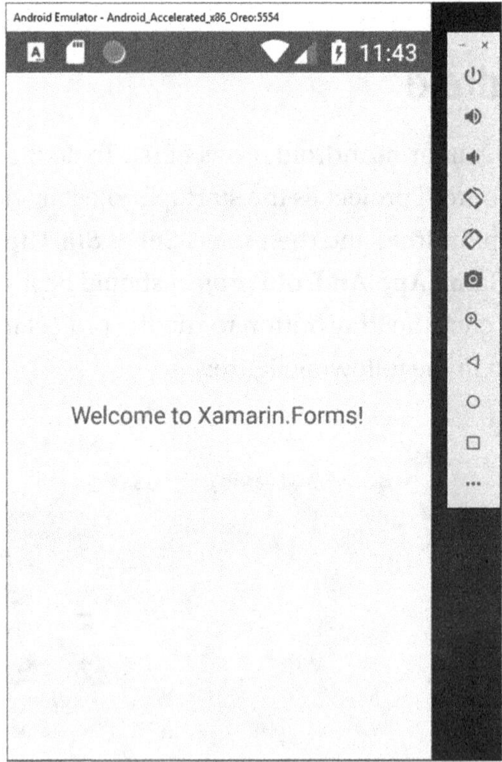

Figure 2-18. *Android emulator output*

The emulator may be left running: it is not necessary to shut it down and wait for it to restart each time the app is launched. The first time a Xamarin.Android app is run in the emulator, the Xamarin.Android shared runtime for the targeted API level is installed, followed by the application. The runtime installation may take a few moments, so please be patient. Installation of the runtime takes place only when the first Xamarin. Android app is deployed to the emulator; subsequent deployments are faster because only the app is copied to the emulator.

At this point, you may close the Android emulator, because we need to test out the **MemoryGame.App.iOS** project.

Xamarin.iOS

To run the Xamarin.iOS project, you need to have a Mac machine to simulate the application. You will first need to pair your Mac so that the **MemoryGame.App.iOS** project can connect to it.

Building native iOS applications requires access to Apple's build tools, which only run on a Mac. Because of this, Visual Studio 2017 must connect to a network-accessible Mac to build Xamarin.iOS applications. For more information on pairing your Mac, see the following:

`https://docs.microsoft.com/en-us/xamarin/ios/get-started/installation/windows/connecting-to-mac/`

Now log on to your Mac machine and then go to **System Preferences ➤ Sharing**. Check the **Remote Login** and select Allow access for: **All users** just like in the following figure:

Figure 2-19. Enabling remote login on Mac

After you've done that, make sure that you have installed **Xcode** on your Mac:

- `https://itunes.apple.com/us/app/xcode/id497799835?mt=12`

Xcode is required in order to build and run iOS apps, so ensure that you installed that correctly and it's functional.

Now go ahead and switch to Visual Studio and set the **MemoryGame.App.iOS** project as a startup project.

Click the **Play** button that says **Simulator** as shown in the following figure.

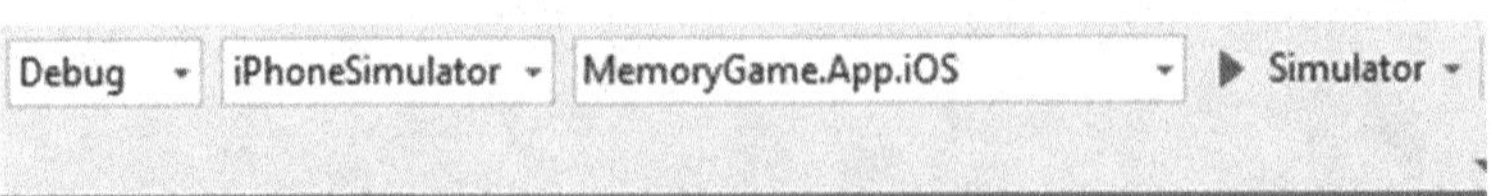

Figure 2-20. Running the Xamarin.iOS project for the first time

Then, it should show the following:

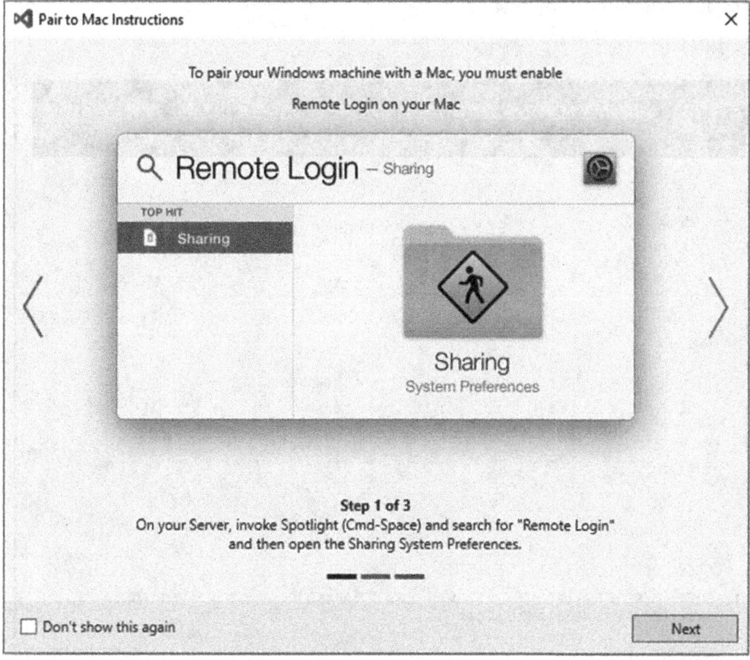

Figure 2-21. *Pair to Mac instructions*

If it is on the same network as the Windows machine, the Mac should now be discoverable by Visual Studio 2017. If the Mac is still not discoverable, try manually adding a Mac or take a look at the troubleshooting guide at the following links:

- `https://docs.microsoft.com/en-us/xamarin/ios/get-started/installation/windows/connecting-to-mac/#manually-add-a-mac`
- `https://docs.microsoft.com/en-us/xamarin/ios/get-started/installation/windows/connecting-to-mac/troubleshooting`

Click **Next** and it should present you with the following screen:

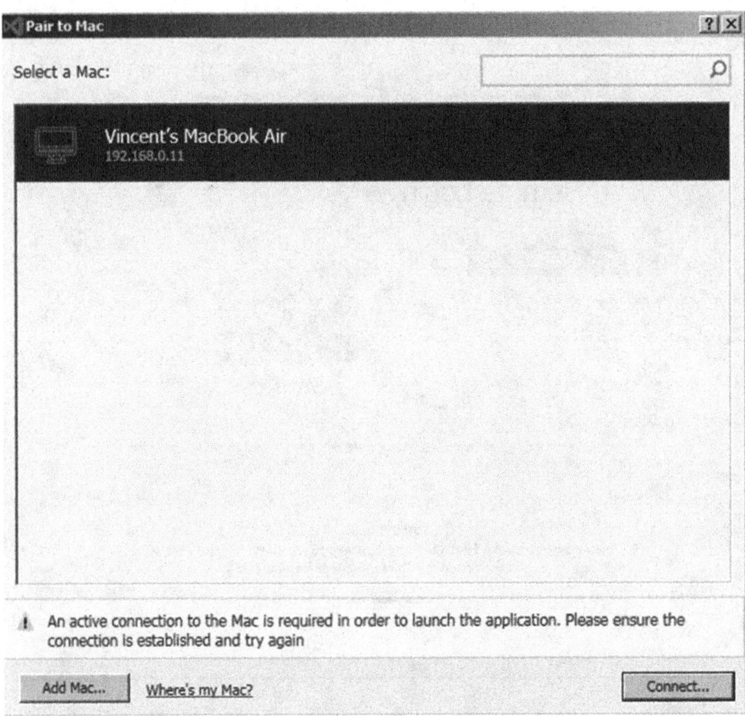

Figure 2-22. *Select a Mac to pair*

Click the **Connect...** button and it should prompt you to provide a username and password for you to connect your Mac machine just like in the following figure:

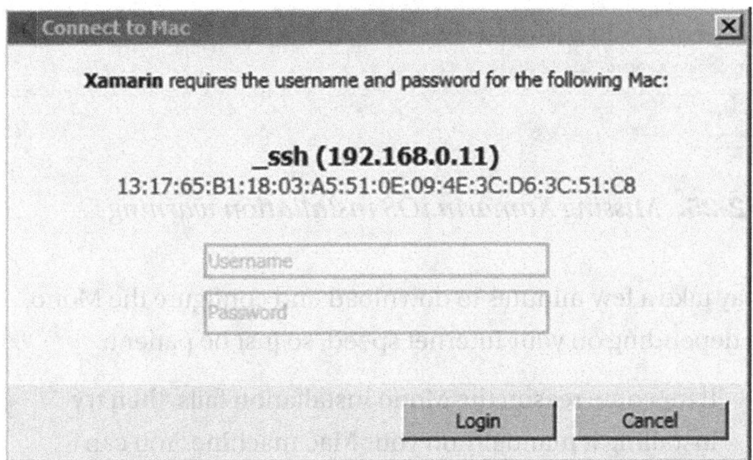

Figure 2-23. *Connect to Mac*

Enter your username and password and click **Login**.

If your login is successful and you are prompted with a Missing Mono installation, simply click **Install** as shown in the following figure:

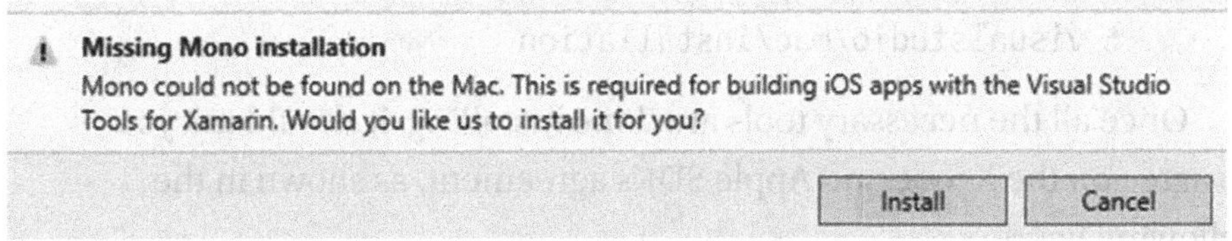

Figure 2-24. *Missing Mono installation warning*

You may also be prompted with the missing Xamarin.iOS installation. Just click Install and it should download and install the missing pieces, as shown in the following figure:

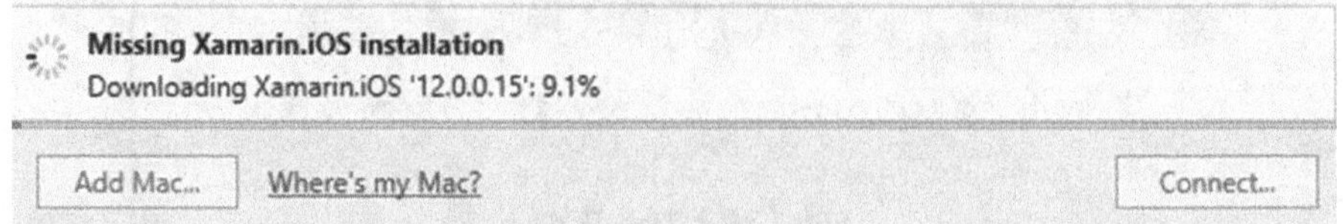

Figure 2-25. *Missing Xamarin.iOS installation warning*

It may take a few minutes to download and configure the Mono settings depending on your Internet speed, so just be patient.

- If for some reason the Mono installation fails, then try installing it manually on your Mac machine. You can download the Mono installer here: `www.mono-project.com/docs/getting-started/install/mac/`
- To ensure that you have everything you need to run Xamarin.iOS on Mac, I would recommend that you install Visual Studio for Mac. You can download the installer here: `https://docs.microsoft.com/en-us/visualstudio/mac/installation`

Once all the necessary tools are done installing, it should ask you to agree on the Xcode and Apple SDKs agreement, as shown in the following figure:

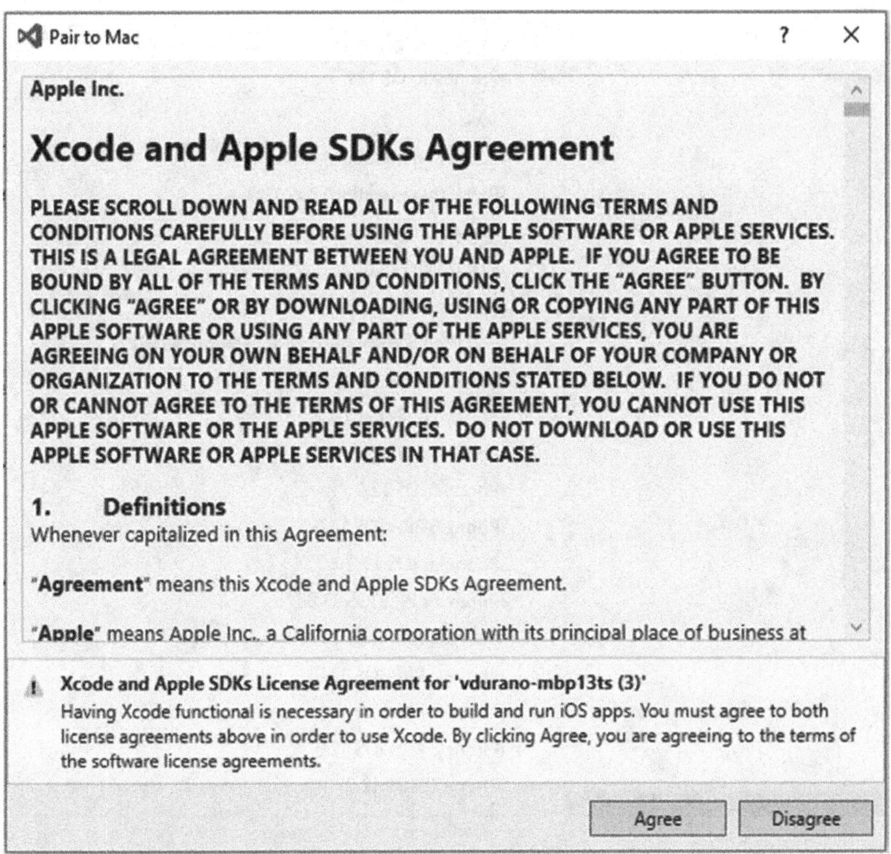

Figure 2-26. *Xcode and Apple SDKs agreement*

Click **Agree**.

Once you your PC is successfully paired to your Mac, then you should be able to see various device emulators in your Visual Studio device list, as shown in the following figure:

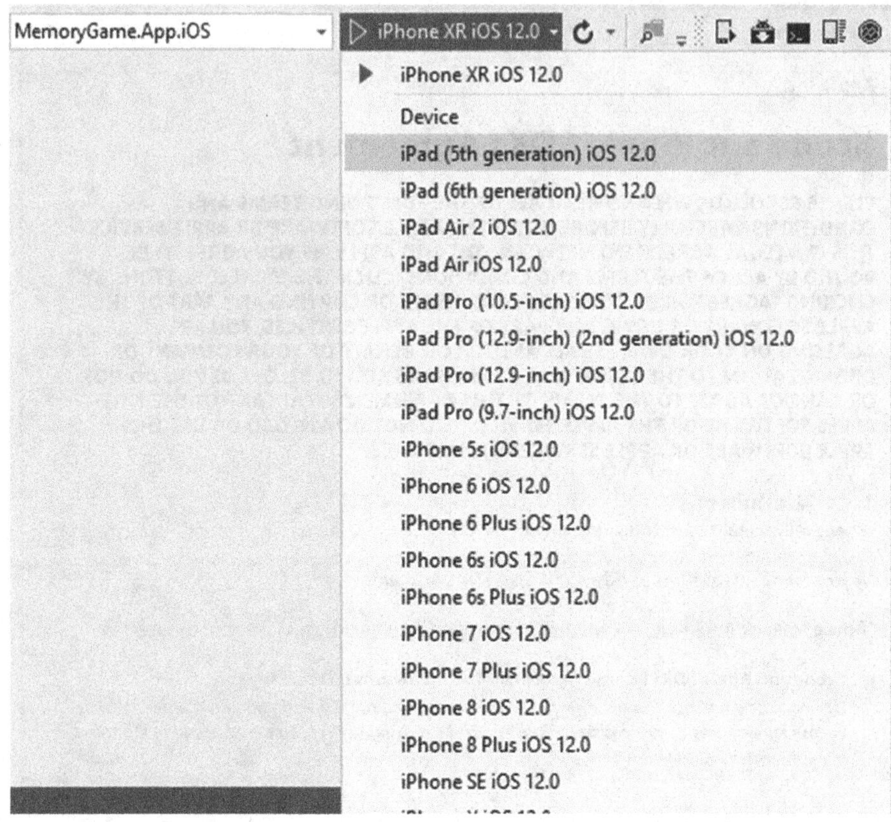

Figure 2-27. *Selecting an iOS device emulator*

Here's a sample screenshot of the Xamarin.iOS running on the iPhone emulator:

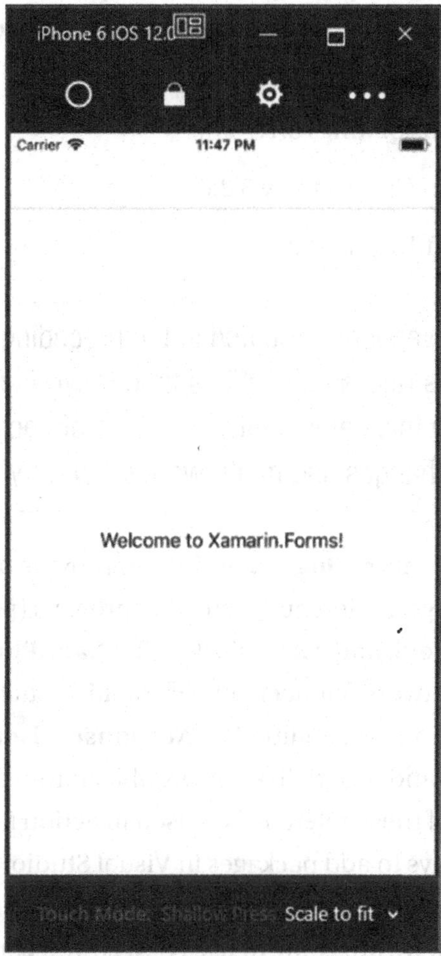

Figure 2-28. *iOS emulator output*

For more information about pairing your PC to Mac, see the following: `https://docs.microsoft.com/en-us/xamarin/ios/get-started/installation/windows/connecting-to-mac/`

The Required NuGet Packages

The next step is adding the packages that are required for our application. Go ahead and right-click the **Solution** and install the following packages in all projects:

- Xam.Plugins.Settings 3.1.1
- Xam.Plugin.Connectivity 3.2.0
- Newtonsoft.Json 11.0.2

Note The specific versions indicated in the preceding. Those are the latest stable versions released as of this time of writing, and we are going to use them in this demo. Future releases of each packages might contain some new changes and might work differently.

We'll be using the **Xam.Plugins.Settings** to provide us consistent cross-platform settings/preferences across all projects (portable library, .NET Standard, Android, and iOS projects). The **Xam.Plugin.Connectivity** will be used to get network connectivity information such as network type, speeds, and connection availability. The **Newtonsoft.Json** will be used in our code to serialize and deserialize a JSON object from an API request. We'll see how each of these references is used in action later.

There are two ways to add packages in Visual Studio; you could either use the Package Manager Console, or proceed via NuGet Package Manager (NPM). In this demo, we are going to use NPM so you can have a visual reference.

Now, right-click the **Solution** level and then select **Manage NuGet Packages for Solution**. Select the **Browse** tab, and in the search bar, type in "Xam.Plugins.Settings". This should result in something like the following:

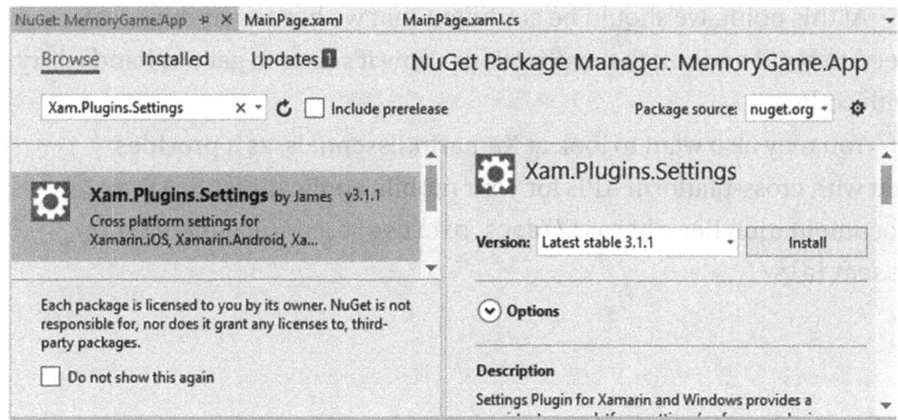

Figure 2-29. *Installing NuGet packages*

When the install is successful, a **reame.txt** file for using the **Xam. Plugins.Settings** should automatically display. Next, install the "**Xam. Plugin.Connectivity**" and "**Newtonsoft.Json**" NuGet packages.

Once you've installed them all, you should be able to see them added in your project **Dependencies** just like in the following figure:

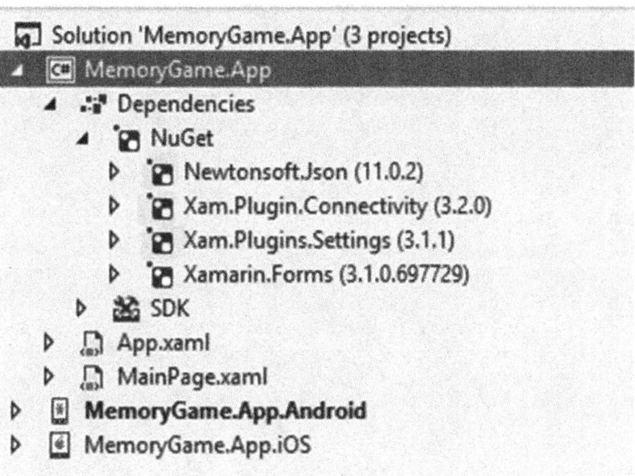

Figure 2-30. *The installed NuGet packages*

At this point, we should be confident that we have everything we need to build and run the applications. Now it's time to get our hands dirty with coding.

You may also want to look at Xamarin.Essentials, as it provides you with cross-platform APIs for your mobile applications. See the documentation here: `https://docs.microsoft.com/en-us/xamarin/essentials/`

CHAPTER 3

Configuring Data Access and API Endpoints

In this chapter, we are going to see in action how to set up a database, configure data access, and build REST API endpoints.

Creating a New Empty Database

Let's start by creating a database for storing and persisting user data. Now go ahead and fire up Microsoft SSMS and just log in using Windows authentication. When you're inside the studio management, select **File ➤ New ➤ Query with Current Connection** just like in the following figure:

V. M. S. Durano, *Understanding Game Application Development*,
https://doi.org/10.1007/978-1-4842-4264-3_3

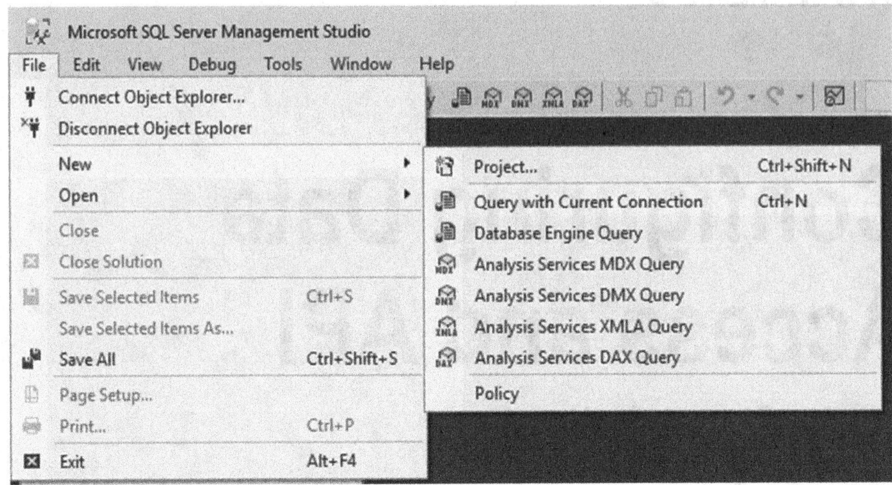

Figure 3-1. *Create a new query editor*

Copy the following SQL script in the query editor:

```
CREATE Database MemoryGame
GO

USE [MemoryGame]
GO

CREATE TABLE [dbo].[Challenger](
       [ChallengerID] [int] IDENTITY(1,1) NOT NULL,
       [FirstName] [varchar](50) NOT NULL,
       [LastName] [varchar](50) NOT NULL,
       [Email] [varchar](50) NULL,
CONSTRAINT [PK_Challenger] PRIMARY KEY CLUSTERED
(
       [ChallengerID] ASC
)WITH (PAD_INDEX  = OFF, STATISTICS_NORECOMPUTE  = OFF,
                    IGNORE_DUP_KEY = OFF,
                    ALLOW_ROW_LOCKS  = ON,
```

```
                    ALLOW_PAGE_LOCKS  = ON)
                    ON [PRIMARY]
) ON [PRIMARY]

GO

CREATE TABLE [dbo].[Rank](
       [RankID] [int] IDENTITY(1,1) NOT NULL,
       [ChallengerID] [int] NOT NULL,
       [Best] [tinyint] NOT NULL,
       [DateAchieved] [datetime] NOT NULL,
 CONSTRAINT [PK_Rank] PRIMARY KEY CLUSTERED
(
       [RankID] ASC
)WITH (PAD_INDEX  = OFF, STATISTICS_NORECOMPUTE  = OFF,
                    IGNORE_DUP_KEY = OFF,
                    ALLOW_ROW_LOCKS  = ON,
                    ALLOW_PAGE_LOCKS  = ON) ON [PRIMARY]
) ON [PRIMARY]

GO
```

Then click the **Execute** button or hit **F5** as shown in the following figure:

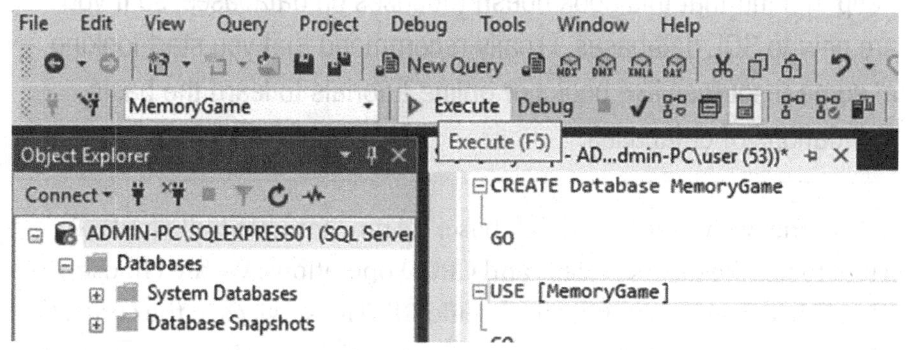

Figure 3-2. *Execute SQL query*

The preceding SQL script should create the "**MemoryGame**" database with the following table:

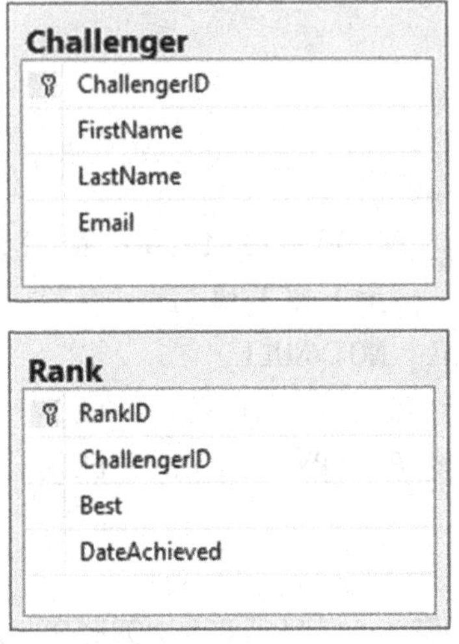

Figure 3-3. *The database schema*

The database tables that we've created are very plain and simple. The **dbo.Challenger** table contains some basic properties for us to identify a user who plays the game. The **dbo.Rank** table similarly contains basic properties to help us identify which user has the highest rank.

Keep in mind that this book doesn't focuses on databases, so if you are new to SQL databases, I really recommend that you start looking at some resources like books or online tutorials to learn the basic foundations of databases.

Now that we've set up our database, it's time for us to build a REST service to handle database calls and CRUD operations. We are choosing Web API because it's a perfect fit to build RESTful services in the context of .NET. It also allows other client apps (mobile apps, web apps, and even desktop apps) to consume our API via endpoints. This would enable our application to allow clients to access data in any type of application as long as it supports HTTP services.

Creating the ASP.NET Web API Project

Let's proceed to our work. Switch back to Visual Studio 2017, add a new project by right-clicking the **Solution** level, and then select **Add ➤ New Project ➤ Visual C# ➤ Web**. Select **ASP.NET Web Application (.NET Framework)** and name the project "**MemoryGame.API**" just like in the following figure:

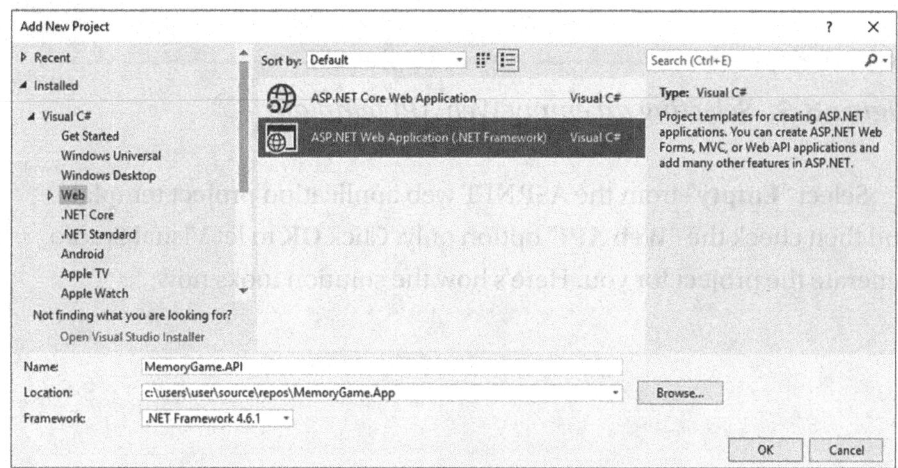

Figure 3-4. *Create a new ASP.NET Web API project*

Click **OK** and you should be presented with the next screen:

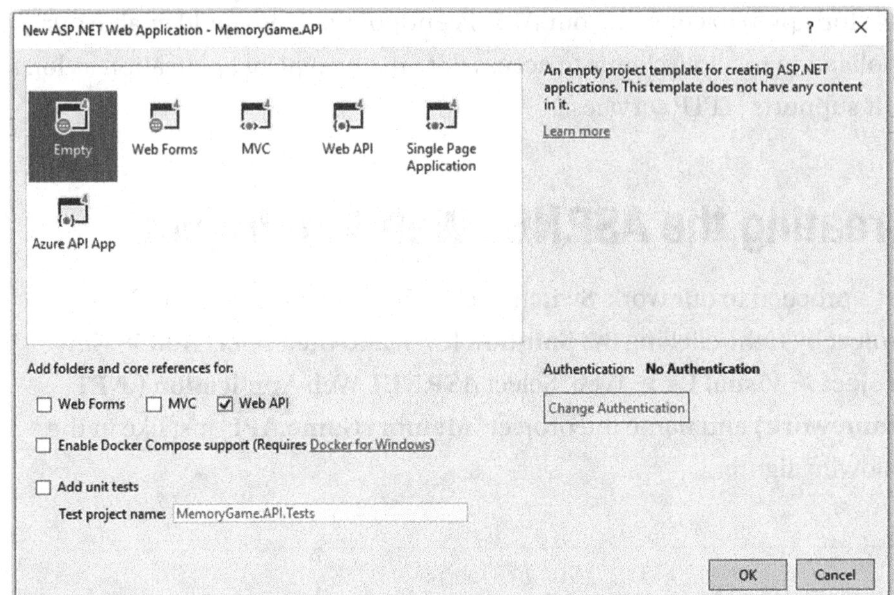

Figure 3-5. *Selecting an empty Web API template*

Select "**Empty**" from the ASP.NET web application project template and then check the "**Web API**" option only. Click **OK** to let Visual Studio generate the project for you. Here's how the solution looks now:

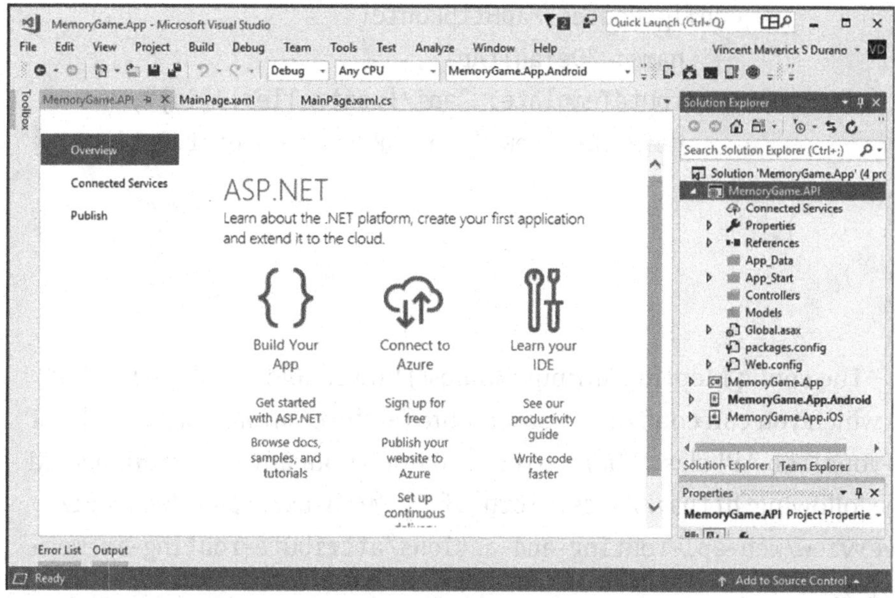

Figure 3-6. *The default generated files*

By default, the ASP.NET Web API project configures a combination of both conventional and attribute-based routing. You can see how the routing is set up by navigating to the **App_Start** folder ➤ **WebApiConfig.cs**. Here's what the code looks like:

```
using System.Web.Http;

namespace MemoryGame.API
{
    public static class WebApiConfig
    {
        public static void Register(HttpConfiguration config)
        {
            // Web API configuration and services

            // Web API routes
            config.MapHttpAttributeRoutes();
```

```
            config.Routes.MapHttpRoute(
                name: "DefaultApi",
                routeTemplate: "api/{controller}/{id}",
                defaults: new { id = RouteParameter.Optional }
            );
        }
    }
}
```

The config.MapHttpAttributeRoutes() line enables attribute routing, in which you can configure custom routes at the controller or action level of your Web API class. For more information about attribute routing, read the following: `https://docs.microsoft.com/en-us/aspnet/web-api/overview/web-api-routing-and-actions/attribute-routing-in-web-api-2`.

The second line of code defines a default route template to the routing table using convention-based routing. Each entry in the routing table contains a route template. The default route template for Web API is "api/{controller}/{id}". In this template, "api" is a literal path segment, and {controller} and {id} are placeholder variables. When the Web API server receives an HTTP request, it tries to match the URI against one of the route templates in the routing table. For more information about conventional routing, read the following: `https://docs.microsoft.com/en-us/aspnet/web-api/overview/web-api-routing-and-actions/routing-in-aspnet-web-api`.

ASP.NET routing is the ability to have URLs represent abstract actions rather than concrete physical files. If you are familiar with ASP.NET MVC, Web API routing is very similar to MVC routing. The main difference is that Web API uses the HTTP method, not the URI path, to select the action.

For this demo, we are going to use attribute routing to add route templates in the routing table because it gives us more flexibility in defining routes than convention routing.

Integrating EF

Now that we have our Web API project ready, let's continue by implementing our data access layer to work with data from database.

In the software development world, most applications require a data store or a database. So, we all need a code to read/write our data stored in a database or a data store. Creating and maintaining code for database make for tedious work and a real challenge. That's where an ORM like EF comes into place.

What Is an ORM?

An ORM enables developers to create data access applications by programming against a conceptual application model instead of programming directly against a relational storage schema. The goal is to decrease the amount of code and maintenance required for data-oriented applications. ORM like EF provides the following benefits:

- Applications can work in terms of a more application-centric conceptual model, including types with inheritance, complex members, and relationships.
- Applications are freed from hard-coded dependencies on a particular data engine or storage schema.
- Mappings between the conceptual model and the storage-specific schema can change without changing the application code.
- Developers can work with a consistent application object model that can be mapped to various storage schemas, possibly implemented in different database management systems.

- Multiple conceptual models can be mapped to a single storage schema.
- Language-integrated query (LINQ) support provides compile-time syntax validation for queries against a conceptual model.

What is EF?

To recap, EF is an ORM that enables .NET developers to work with relational data using domain-specific objects. It eliminates the need for most of the data access code that developers usually need to write.

This could simply mean that using EF we will be working with entities (class/object representation of your data structure) and letting the framework handle the basic create, read, udpate, and delete (CRUD) operations. In traditional ADO.NET, you will write the SQL queries directly against tables/columns/procedures and you don't have entities, so it's much less object oriented.

For more information, read the following: `https://msdn.microsoft.com/en-us/library/aa937723(v=vs.113).aspx`.

Just like any other ORM, there are two main design workflows supported by EF: In the **Code-First** approach, you create your classes (POCO entities) and generate a new database out from them. The **Database-First** approach allows you to use an existing database and generate classes based on your database schema. For this demo, we're going to use a Database-First approach, as we already have an existing database created.

Setting Up a Data Access Layer

In the **MemoryGame.API** project, create a new folder called "**DB**" under the **Models** folder. Within the "**DB**" folder, add an **ADO.NET Entity Data Model**. To do this, just follow these steps:

1. Right-click the "**DB**" folder and then select **Add ➤ New Item**.
2. On the left pane under **Visual C#** item, select **Data ➤ ADO.NET Entity Data Model**.
3. Name the file as "**MemoryGameDB**" and then click **Add**.
4. In the next wizard, select **EF Designer** from **Database** and then click **Next**.
5. Click the "**New Connection...**" button.
6. Select **Microsoft SQL Server** under **Data source** and click **Continue**.
7. Supply the database server name to where you created the database. In my case, the name of my SQL server is "ADMIN-PC\SQLEXPRESS01". Remember that yours can be different, so make sure you supply the correct instance. You can find the server name in SSMS.
8. Select or enter the database name. In this case, the database name for this example is "**MemoryGame**".
9. Click the T**est Connection** button to see if it's successful just like in the following figure:

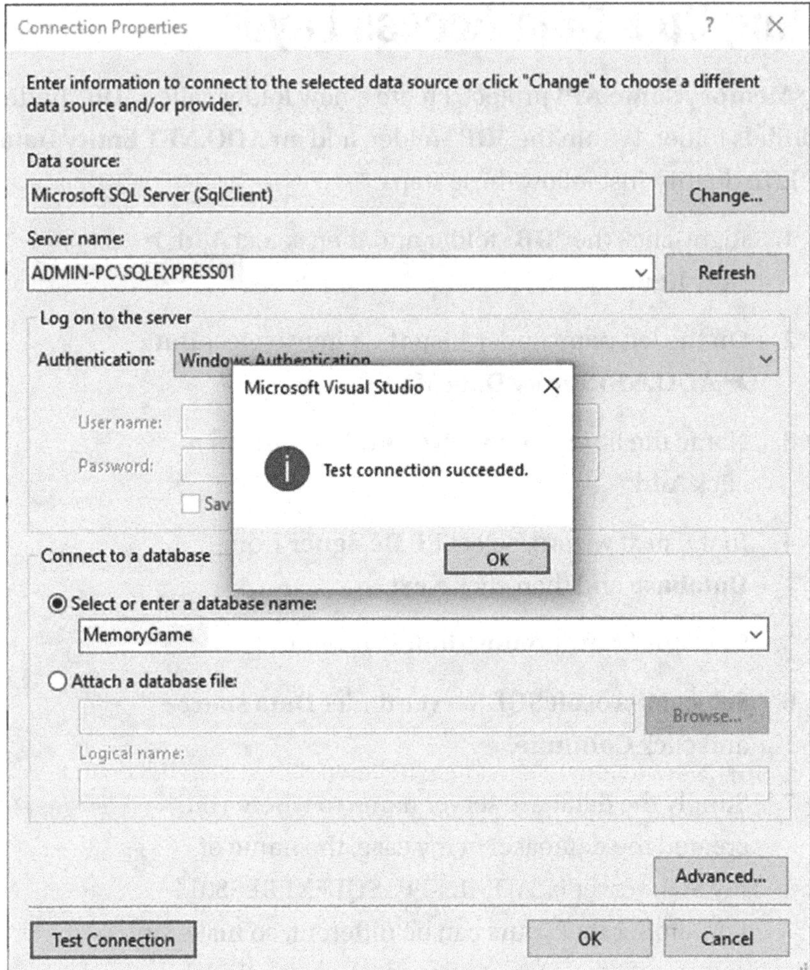

***Figure 3-7.** Testing the database connection*

10. Click **OK** to close the pop-up dialog and click **OK** again to generate the connection string that will be used for our application.

11. In the next wizard, click **Next**.

12. Select **EF 6.x** and then click **Next**.

13. Select the "**Challenger**" and "**Rank**" tables and then click **Finish**.

The **.EDMX** file should now be added under the "**DB**" folder just like in the following figure:

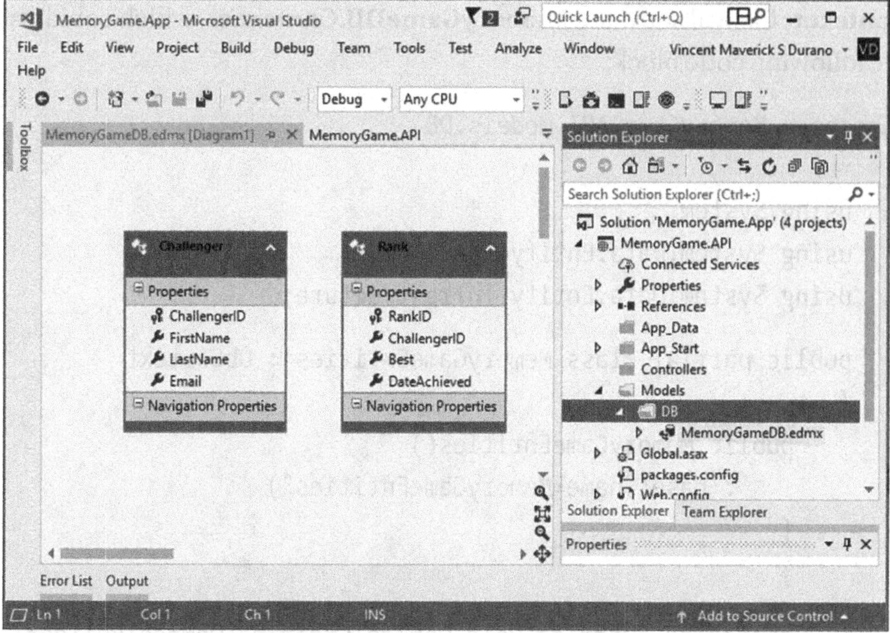

Figure 3-8. *The generated entity models*

What happens there is that EF automatically generates the business objects for you and lets you query against it. The EDMX or the entity data model will serve as the main gateway by which you retrieve objects from the database and resubmit changes.

Under the hood, the EDMX file contains the following child files:

- MemoryGameDB.Context.tt
- MemoryGameDB.Designer.cs

- MemoryGameDB.Edmx.diagram
- MemoryGameDB.tt

The **MemoryGameDB.Context.tt** is a Visual Studio text template file (a.k.a. **T4** template). A T4 text template is a mixture of text blocks and control logic that can generate a text file. The control logic is written as fragments of program code in Visual C#. Expanding the **MemoryGameDB.Context.tt** file will show the **MemoryGameDB.Context.cs**, which contains the following code block:

```
namespace MemoryGame.API.Models.DB
{
    using System;
    using System.Data.Entity;
    using System.Data.Entity.Infrastructure;

    public partial class MemoryGameEntities : DbContext
    {
        public MemoryGameEntities()
            : base("name=MemoryGameEntities")
        {
        }

        protected override void OnModelCreating(DbModelBuilder
        modelBuilder)
        {
            throw new UnintentionalCodeFirstException();
        }

        public virtual DbSet<Challenger> Challengers { get; set; }
        public virtual DbSet<Rank> Ranks { get; set; }
    }
}
```

The **MemoryGameEntities** class represents a session with the database and allows you to query and save instances of the entity classes. This class derives from **DbContext** and exposes **DbSet** virtual properties that represent collections of the specified entities in the context. Since we are working with the EF Designer (EDMX), the context is automatically generated for us. If you are working with the Code-First approach, you will typically write the context yourself.

You may have noticed that the models generated are created as partial classes. This means that you can extend them by creating another partial class for each of the entity model classes when necessary.

Once you have a model, the primary class your application interacts with is **System.Data.Entity.DbContext** (often referred to as the context class). You can use a **DbContext** associated to a model to:

- Write and execute queries
- Materialize query results as entity objects
- Track changes that are made to those objects
- Persist object changes back on the database
- Bind objects in memory to UI controls

The **MemoryGameDB.tt** contains the following generated classes based from the table we defined from the database:

- Challenger.cs

```
namespace MemoryGame.API.Models.DB
{
    using System;
    using System.Collections.Generic;

    public partial class Challenger
    {
        public int ChallengerID { get; set; }
```

```
        public string FirstName { get; set; }
        public string LastName { get; set; }
        public string Email { get; set; }
    }
}
```

- Rank.cs

```
namespace MemoryGame.API.Models.DB
{
    using System;
    using System.Collections.Generic;

    public partial class Rank
    {
        public int RankID { get; set; }
        public int ChallengerID { get; set; }
        public byte Best { get; set; }
        public System.DateTime DateAchieved { get; set; }
    }
}
```

The classes generated in the preceding will be used as a type of DbSet objects. The **DbSet** class represents an entity set that can be used for CRUD operations.

The **DbSet** class is derived from **IQuerayable**. So, we can use LINQ for querying against **DbSet**, which will be converted to a SQL query. EF API executes this SQL query to the underlying database, gets the flat result set, converts it into appropriate entity objects, and returns it as a query result.

Implementing CRUD Operations

The next step is to create a central class for handling CRUD operations. Now, create a new folder called "**DataManager**" under the **Models** folder. Right-click the **DataManager** folder and select **Add ➤ New ➤ Class.** Name the class as "**GameManager**", click the **Add** button, and then copy the following code:

```
using System;
using System.Collections.Generic;
using System.Linq;
using MemoryGame.API.Models.DB;

namespace MemoryGame.API.Models.DataManager
{

    #region DTO
    public class ChallengerViewModel
    {
        public int ChallengerID { get; set; }
        public string FirstName { get; set; }
        public string LastName { get; set; }
        public byte Best { get; set; }
        public DateTime DateAchieved { get; set; }
    }
    #endregion

    #region HTTP Response Object
    public class HTTPApiResponse
    {
        public enum StatusResponse
        {
            Success = 1,
            Fail = 2
        }
```

```
        public StatusResponse Status { get; set; }
        public string StatusDescription { get; set; }
        public int StatusCode { get; set; }
    }
    #endregion

    #region Data Access
    public class GameManager
    {

        public IEnumerable<ChallengerViewModel> GetAll { get {
        return GetAllChallengerRank(); } }

        public List<ChallengerViewModel> GetAllChallengerRank()
        {
            using (MemoryGameEntities db = new
            MemoryGameEntities())
            {
                var result = (from c in db.Challengers
                              join r in db.Ranks on
                              c.ChallengerID equals
                              r.ChallengerID
                              select new ChallengerViewModel
                              {
                                 ChallengerID = c.ChallengerID,
                                 FirstName = c.FirstName,
                                 LastName = c.LastName,
                                 Best = r.Best,
                                 DateAchieved = r.DateAchieved
                              }).OrderByDescending(o => o.Best)
                              .ThenBy(o => o.DateAchieved);

                return result.ToList();
            }
```

```
}
public HTTPApiResponse UpdateCurrentBest(DB.Rank user)
{
    using (MemoryGameEntities db = new MemoryGameEntities())
    {
        var data = db.Ranks.Where(o => o.ChallengerID
        == user.ChallengerID);
        if (data.Any())
        {
            Rank rank = data.FirstOrDefault();
            rank.Best = user.Best;
            rank.DateAchieved = user.DateAchieved;
            db.SaveChanges();
        }
        else
        {
            db.Ranks.Add(user);
            db.SaveChanges();
        }
    }

    return new HTTPApiResponse
    {
        Status = HTTPApiResponse.StatusResponse.Success,
        StatusCode = 200,
        StatusDescription = "Operation successful."
    };
}

public int GetChallengerID(string email)
{
    using (MemoryGameEntities db = new MemoryGameEntities())
    {
```

```
                var data = db.Challengers.Where(o => o.Email.
                ToLower().Equals(email.ToLower()));
                if (data.Any())
                {
                    return data.FirstOrDefault().ChallengerID;
                }

                return 0;
            }
        }

        public HTTPApiResponse AddChallenger(DB.Challenger c)
        {
            HTTPApiResponse response = null;
            using (MemoryGameEntities db = new MemoryGameEntities())
            {
                var data = db.Challengers.Where(o => o.Email.
                ToLower().Equals(c.Email.ToLower()));
                if (data.Any())
                {
                    response = new HTTPApiResponse
                    {
                        Status = HTTPApiResponse.
                                 StatusResponse.Fail,
                        StatusCode = 400,
                        StatusDescription = "User with
                        associated email already exist."
                    };
                }
                else
                {
                    db.Challengers.Add(c);
                    db.SaveChanges();
```

```
                response = new HTTPApiResponse
                {
                    Status = HTTPApiResponse.StatusResponse.
                    Success,
                    StatusCode = 200,
                    StatusDescription = "Operation successful."
                };
            }

            return response;
        }
    }

    public ChallengerViewModel GetChallengerByEmail(string
    email)
{
    using (MemoryGameEntities db = new MemoryGameEntities())
    {
        var result = (from c in db.Challengers
                      join r in db.Ranks on c.ChallengerID
                      equals r.ChallengerID
                      where c.Email.ToLower().Equals(email.
                      ToLower())
                      select new ChallengerViewModel
                      {
                          ChallengerID = c.ChallengerID,
                          FirstName = c.FirstName,
                          LastName = c.LastName,
                          Best = r.Best,
                          DateAchieved = r.DateAchieved
                      });
```

```
            if (result.Any())
                return result.SingleOrDefault();
        }

        return new ChallengerViewModel();
    }

    public HTTPApiResponse DeleteChallenger(int id)
    {

        HTTPApiResponse response = null;
        using (MemoryGameEntities db = new MemoryGameEntities())
        {
            var data = db.Challengers.Where(o => o.ChallengerID == id);
            if (data.Any())
            {
                try
                {
                    var rankData = db.Ranks.Where(o =>
                    o.ChallengerID == id);
                    if (rankData.Any())
                    {
                        db.Ranks.Remove(rankData.FirstOrDefault());
                        db.SaveChanges();
                    }

                    db.Challengers.Remove(data.FirstOrDefault());
                    db.SaveChanges();

                    response = new HTTPApiResponse
                    {
                        Status = HTTPApiResponse.
                        StatusResponse.Success,
                        StatusCode = 200,
```

```
                    StatusDescription = "Operation successful."
                };
            }
            catch (System.Data.Entity.Validation.
            DbUnexpected ValidationException)
            {
                //handle error and log

                response = new HTTPApiResponse
                {
                    Status = HTTPApiResponse.StatusResponse.Fail,
                    StatusCode = 500,
                    StatusDescription = "An unexpected
                    error occurred."
                    };
                }
            }
            else
            {
                response = new HTTPApiResponse
                {
                    Status = HTTPApiResponse.StatusResponse.Fail,
                    StatusCode = 400,
                    StatusDescription = "Associated ID not found."
                };
            }

            return response;

        }
    }
}
#endregion
}
```

Let's take a look of what we just did there.

The preceding code is composed of three main regions: The Data Transfer Object (DTO), the HTTP Response Object, and the GameMananger class. Let's break this down into code details. We will start with the DTO:

```
public class ChallengerViewModel
{
    public int ChallengerID { get; set; }
    public string FirstName { get; set; }
    public string LastName { get; set; }
    public byte Best { get; set; }
    public DateTime DateAchieved { get; set; }
}
```

The **ChallengerViewModel** DTO is nothing but a plain class that houses some properties that will be used in the view or any client that consumes the API.

Next code block:

```
public class HTTPApiResponse
{
    public enum StatusResponse
    {
        Success = 1,
        Fail = 2
    }

    public StatusResponse Status { get; set; }
    public string StatusDescription { get; set; }
    public int StatusCode { get; set; }
}
```

The **HTTPApiResponse** object is class that holds an enum and three main basic properties: **Status**, **StatusCode**, and **StatusDescription**. This object will be used in the **GameManager** class methods as a response or return type object.

The **GameManager** class is the central class where we handle the actual CRUD operations. This is where we use EF to communicate with the database by working with a conceptual data entity instead of a real SQL query. EF enables us to work with a database using .NET objects and eliminates the need for most of the data access code that developers usually need to write.

Let's break this down into code details. Let's start with this code:

```
public IEnumerable<ChallengerViewModel> GetAll { get { return
GetAllChallengerRank(); } }
```

The method **GetAll** is a public property that returns an **IEnumerable <ChallengerViewModel>**. The sole purpose of this property is to get the data; that is why we only set a getter accessor. Creating a property with only a getter makes your property read-only for any code that is outside the class.

Next code block:

```
public List<ChallengerViewModel> GetAllChallengerRank()
{
    using (MemoryGameEntities db = new MemoryGameEntities())
    {
        var result = (from c in db.Challengers
                      join r in db.Ranks on c.ChallengerID
                      equals r.ChallengerID
                      select new ChallengerViewModel
                      {
                          ChallengerID = c.ChallengerID,
                          FirstName = c.FirstName,
```

```
                              LastName = c.LastName,
                              Best = r.Best,
                              DateAchieved = r.DateAchieved
                          }).OrderByDescending(o => o.Best)
                          .ThenBy(o => o.DateAchieved);

        return result.ToList();
    }
}
```

The method **GetAllChallengerRank()** basically fetches the challenger's profile and its corresponding rank. The first line of the code within the method creates an instance of the **DbContext** called **MemoryGameEntities**. We wrap the code for instantiating the **DbContext** within the **using** block to ensure that the objects will be properly disposed of after using them.

The next line uses a LINQ query expression to query the data. The query joins the **db.Challenger** and **db.Rank** DbSets using the **join** clause. We then **select** the data that we need and associate them into a strongly typed object called ChallengerViewModel, order the results by highest rank, and return the result by calling the ToList() function. **ToList()** is an extension method that sits within the **System.Linq** namespace, which converts collections (IEnumerables) to list instances.

Next code block:

```
public HTTPApiResponse UpdateCurrentBest(DB.Rank user)
{
    using (MemoryGameEntities db = new MemoryGameEntities())
    {
        var data = db.Ranks.Where(o => o.ChallengerID ==
        user.ChallengerID);
```

```
        if (data.Any())
        {
            Rank rank = data.FirstOrDefault();
            rank.Best = user.Best;
            rank.DateAchieved = user.DateAchieved;
            db.SaveChanges();
        }
        else
        {
            db.Ranks.Add(user);
            db.SaveChanges();
        }
    }

    return new HTTPApiResponse
    {
        Status = HTTPApiResponse.StatusResponse.Success,
        StatusCode = 200,
        StatusDescription = "Operation successful."
    };
}
```

The **UpdateCurrentBest()** method takes the **DB.Rank** class as the parameter. The code block basically gets the **Rank** object based on the **ChallengerID** using the LINQ **Where** function and assigns the result into a variable **data**. We then call the LINQ **Any()** function to check if the object contains any single element in a sequence.

If there's any data returned from the query, then we create an instance of the **Rank** class and set the result from the **data** variable using the FirstOrDefault() LINQ function. The LINQ **FirstOrDefault()**is an eager function that returns the first element of a sequence that satisfies a specified condition. Once the FirstOrDefault() function is invoked,

EF will automatically issue a parameterize SQL query to the database, in which the SQL Server can understand and then bring back the result to the entity model. We then assign the new values to each field and call the **SaveChanges()** method to update the database with the changes.

Otherwise, if there's no data or if the LINQ **Any()** function returns false, then we simply create a new record in the database.

Finally, we return an **HTTPApiResponse** object indicating that the operation is successful.

Next code block:

```
public int GetChallengerID(string email)
{
    using (MemoryGameEntities db = new MemoryGameEntities())
    {
        var data = db.Challengers.Where(o => o.Email.ToLower().
        Equals(email.ToLower()));
        if (data.Any())
        {
            return data.FirstOrDefault().ChallengerID;
        }

        return 0;
    }
}
```

As the method name suggests, the **GetChallengerID()** method gets the **ChallengerID** of the challenger by passing an e-mail as the parameter. The preceding code may be familiar to you by now, as it uses common LINQ functions that we previously talked about such as the **Where()**, **Any()**, and **FirstOrDefault()**.

Next code block:

```
public HTTPApiResponse AddChallenger(DB.Challenger c)
{
    HTTPApiResponse response = null;
    using (MemoryGameEntities db = new MemoryGameEntities())
    {
        var data = db.Challengers.Where(o => o.Email.ToLower().
        Equals(c.Email.ToLower()));
        if (data.Any())
        {
            response = new HTTPApiResponse
            {
                Status = HTTPApiResponse.StatusResponse.Fail,
                StatusCode = 400,
                StatusDescription = "User with associated email
                already exist."
            };
        }
        else
        {
            db.Challengers.Add(c);
            db.SaveChanges();

            response = new HTTPApiResponse
            {
                Status = HTTPApiResponse.StatusResponse.Success,
                StatusCode = 200,
                StatusDescription = "Operation successful."
            };
        }
```

```
        return response;
    }
}
```

The **AddChallengerID()** method takes a **DB.Challenger** class. The preceding code checks if the data associated with the e-mail already exists in the database. If it does, then it returns an error; otherwise it adds a new entry to the database and returns a successful response.

Next code block:

```
public ChallengerViewModel GetChallengerByEmail(string email)
{
    using (MemoryGameEntities db = new MemoryGameEntities())
    {
        var result = (from c in db.Challengers
                      join r in db.Ranks on c.ChallengerID
                      equals r.ChallengerID
                      where c.Email.ToLower().Equals(email.
                      ToLower())
                      select new ChallengerViewModel
                      {
                          ChallengerID = c.ChallengerID,
                          FirstName = c.FirstName,
                          LastName = c.LastName,
                          Best = r.Best,
                          DateAchieved = r.DateAchieved
                      });

        if (result.Any())
            return result.SingleOrDefault();
    }

    return new ChallengerViewModel();
}
```

The code implementation of **GetChallengerByEmail()** function is somewhat similar to the **GetAllChallengerRank()** function. The only difference is that we filter the data by e-mail using the LINQ **Where()** function, and this returns only a single result using the LINQ **SingleOrDefault()** function. The **SingleOrDefault()** function is similar to **FirstOrDefault()** in the sense of returning just a single row. However, they differ in terms of how they are used. Whenever you use SingleOrDefault(), you clearly state that the query should result in at most a single result. On the other hand, when **FirstOrDefault()** is used, the query can return any number of results, but you state that you only want the first one. Since we let e-mail be unique, we are sure that e-mails can't be duplicated, and thus we opt for **SingleOrDefault()**.

Next code block:

```
public HTTPApiResponse DeleteChallenger(int id)
{
    HTTPApiResponse response = null;
    using (MemoryGameEntities db = new MemoryGameEntities())
    {
        var data = db.Challengers.Where(o => o.ChallengerID == id);
        if (data.Any())
        {
            try
            {
                var rankData = db.Ranks.Where(o =>
                o.ChallengerID == id);
                if (rankData.Any())
                {
                    db.Ranks.Remove(rankData.FirstOrDefault());
                    db.SaveChanges();
                }
```

```
                db.Challengers.Remove(data.FirstOrDefault());
                db.SaveChanges();

                response = new HTTPApiResponse
                {
                Status = HTTPApiResponse.StatusResponse.
                Success,
                StatusCode = 200,
                StatusDescription = "Operation successful."
            };
        }
        catch (System.Data.Entity.Validation.DbUnexpected
        ValidationException)
        {
            //handle error and log

            response = new HTTPApiResponse
            {
                Status = HTTPApiResponse.StatusResponse.Fail,
                StatusCode = 500,
                StatusDescription = "An unexpected error occurred."
            };
        }
    }
    else
    {
        response = new HTTPApiResponse
        {
            Status = HTTPApiResponse.StatusResponse.Fail,
            StatusCode = 400,
            StatusDescription = "Associated ID not found."
        };
    }
```

```
        return response;
    }
}
```

The **DeleteChallenger()** method takes an **id** as the parameter. This means it deletes all information for a certain challenger and its associated rank. The code basically checks for the existence of the challenger by querying the database using the LINQ **Where()** function. If the record exists, then it will delete the record that is associated with the **id** in both the **Rank** and **Challenger** database tables. Otherwise, it returns a response saying the associated ID was not found.

To summarize, the **GameManager** class is composed of the following methods:

- **GetAll()** - A short method that calls the **GetAllChallengerRank()** method and returns an **IEnumerable<ChallengerViewModel>**.
- **GetAllChallengerRank()** - Gets all the challenger names and their corresponding ranks. It uses LINQ to query the model and sort the data. This method returns a **List<ChallengerViewModel>** object.
- **GetChallengerByEmail(string email)** - Gets the challenger information and its corresponding rank by e-mail. This method returns a **ChallengerViewModel** object.
- **GetChallengerID(string email)** - Gets the challenger ID by passing an e-mail address as parameter. This method returns an int type.
- **AddChallenger(DB.Challenger c)** - Adds a new challenger to the database. This method returns an HTTPApiResponse object.

- **UpdateCurrentBest(DB.Rank user)** - Updates the rank of a challenger to the newly achieved high score. This method returns an **HTTPApiResponse** object.
- **DeleteChallenger(int id)** - Deletes a challenger from the database. This method returns an HTTPApiResponse object.

A Friendly Reminder

It was my intent not to decouple the actual implementation of the data access layer, as I'm trying to make this demo as simple as possible. In a real-world scenario where you want to deal with a complex database and value the testability of your data access, then I'd recommend you implement a data repository pattern. The main reason for adding your own repository implementation is so that you can use **DependencyInjection** (DI) and make your code more testable. EF is not that testable out of the box, but it's quite easy to make a mockable version of the EF data context with an **Interface** that can be injected. In other words, if you implement an interface for your data access, other services such as Web API can just use that interface instead of directly accessing your **DBContext** from your Web API controller.

The Web API Endpoints

Now that we have our data access ready, we can start creating the API endpoints to serve data using ASP.NET Web API. As a recap, Web API is a framework used to build HTTP services and is an ideal platform for building RESTful applications on the .NET Framework.

Create a new folder called "**API**" within the root of the **MemoryGame.API** application. Right-click the API folder and select **Add ➤ Controller**. Select **Web API 2 Controller - Empty** just like in the following figure:

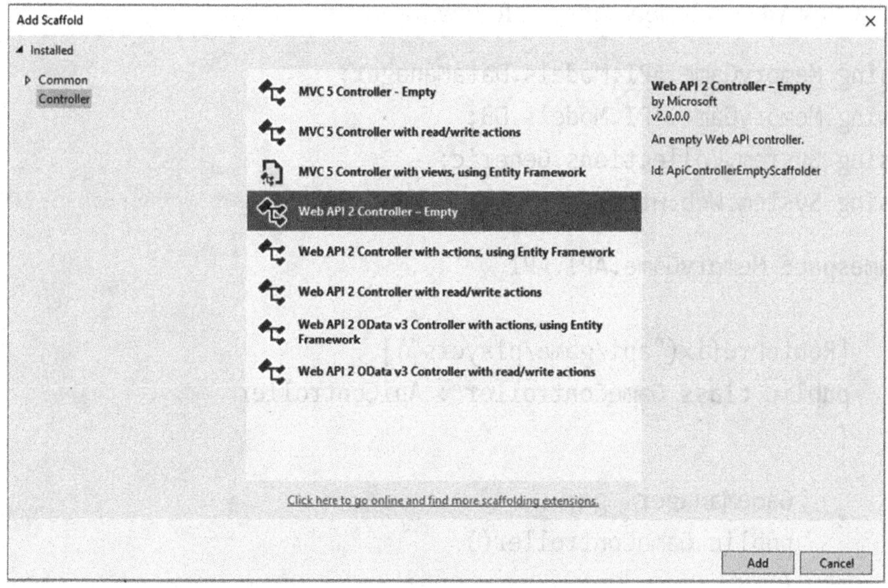

Figure 3-9. *Adding a new empty Web API 2 controller*

Click **Add** and then, on the next screen, name the controller "**GameController**" like in the following figure:

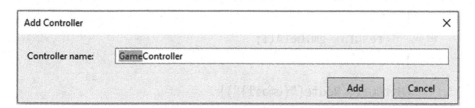

Figure 3-10. *Assigning the controller name*

Click **Add** and then copy the following code:

```
using MemoryGame.API.Models.DataManager;
using MemoryGame.API.Models.DB;
using System.Collections.Generic;
using System.Web.Http;

namespace MemoryGame.API.API
{
    [RoutePrefix("api/game/players")]
    public class GameController : ApiController
    {

        GameManager _gm;
        public GameController()
        {
            _gm = new GameManager();
        }

        [HttpGet, Route("")]
        public IEnumerable<ChallengerViewModel> Get()
        {
            return _gm.GetAll;
        }

        [HttpGet, Route("{email}")]
        public int GetPlayerID(string email)
        {
            return _gm.GetChallengerID(email);
        }

        [HttpGet, Route("~/api/game/profile/{email}")]
        public ChallengerViewModel GetPlayerProfile(string email)
```

```
        {
            return _gm.GetChallengerByEmail(email);
        }

        [HttpPost, Route("")]
        public HTTPApiResponse AddPlayer(Challenger user)
        {
            return _gm.AddChallenger(user);
        }

        [Route("score")]
        [HttpPost]
        public void UpdateScore(Rank user)
        {
            _gm.UpdateCurrentBest(user);
        }

        [HttpDelete, Route("{id}")]
        public HTTPApiResponse DeletePlayer(int id)
        {
            return _gm.DeleteChallenger(id);
        }

    }
}
```

The preceding code comprises the Web API endpoint definitions. It uses an **Attribute Routing** for defining routes that maps to the actual code implementation of the endpoint. Let's break down the code details. We will start at the class level with the following code:

```
[RoutePrefix("api/game/players")]
public class GameController : ApiController
{
    //trimmed down code for clarity
}
```

The **GameController** class is the main entry point for the API endpoints. This class derives the **ApiController** class and uses the **RoutePrefix** attribute for defining a common prefix for all routes within the class. In this demo, the common route prefix is "api/game/players".

ApiControllers contain methods and properties that are specialized in returning data. For example, they take care of transparently serializing the data into the format requested by the client. Also, they follow a different routing scheme by default (as in: mapping URLs to actions), providing a RESTful API by convention.

> *If you have worked with ASP.NET MVC, then you are already familiar with controllers. They work similarly in Web API, but controllers in Web API derive from the ApiController class instead of the controller class. The first major difference you will notice is that actions on Web API controllers do not return views, they return data.*

Next code block:

```
GameManager _gm;
public GameController()
{
    _gm = new GameManager();
}
```

This code is the class constructor of the **GameController** class. This is where we initialize the creation of the **GameManager** class instance. The **GameManager** is the data access gateway, which contains the methods for handling CRUD operations. Just to remind you again, you may want to implement an **Interface** to decouple the **GameManager** object from your Web API controller to make your class more testable.

Next code block:

```
[HttpGet, Route("")]
public IEnumerable<ChallengerViewModel> Get()
{
    return _gm.GetAll;
}
```

The **Get()** method fetches all challenger data from the database and returns an **IEnumerable<ChallengerViewModel>**. Notice that the method is decorated with the **[HttpGet]** and [**Route]** attributes. This means that this method can be invoked only on a **GET** Http request and routes to "api/game/players". Setting the route attribute to empty (**[Route("")]**) automatically maps to the base route defined at the class level.

Next code block:

```
[HttpGet, Route("{email}")]
public int GetPlayerID(string email)
{
    return _gm.GetChallengerID(email);
}
```

The **GetPlayerID()** method takes an e-mail as the parameter. This method invokes the **GetChallengerID()** from the **GameChallenger** class, which returns the **ID** of a challenger that is associated in the e-mail. This method can be invoked only on a **GET** Http request, as we are decorating the method with the **[HttpGet]** attribute. The **{email}** value in the route is the parameter template holder that maps to the **string email** parameter of the **GetPlayerID()** method. This method routes to the following endpoint: "api/game/players/testemail.com/", where "testemail.com" is the value of e-mail passed to the route template.

Next code block:

```
[HttpGet, Route("profile/{email}")]
public ChallengerViewModel GetPlayerProfile(string email)
{
    return _gm.GetChallengerByEmail(email);
}
```

The **GetPlayerProfile()** method also takes an e-mail as the parameter and invokes the **GetChallengerByEmail()** method from the **GameManager** class. This method can be invoked only on a **GET** Http request, as we are decorating the method with the **[HttpGet]** attribute. This method routes to "api/game/players/profile/testemail.com/", where "testemail.com" is the value of e-mail passed to the route template.

Next code block:

```
[HttpPost, Route("")]
public HTTPApiResponse SavePlayer(Challenger user)
{
    return _gm.SaveChallenger(user);
}
```

The **SavePlayer()** method takes a **Challenger** model as the parameter and creates a new entry into the database. This method invokes the **SaveChallenger()** method from the **GameManager** class and returns an **HTTPApiResponse** object. Notice that the method is now decorated with the **[HttpPost]**. This means that this method can be invoked only on a **POST** Http request and routes to base endpoint "api/game/players".

Next code block:

```
[HttpPost, Route("score")]
public void AddScore(Rank user)
{
    _gm.UpdateCurrentBest(user);
}
```

The **AddScore()** method takes a **Rank** model as the parameter and creates or updates the current best score of the challenger record in the database. This method invokes the **UpdateCurrentBest()** method from the **GameManager** class and returns **void**. This method can be invoked only on a **POST** Http request, and it routes to "api/game/players/score".

Next code block:

```
[HttpDelete, Route("{id}")]
public HTTPApiResponse DeletePlayer(int id)
{
    return _gm.DeleteChallenger(id);
}
```

The **DeletePlayer()** method takes an **integer** value as the parameter and deletes the challenger profile and associated rank record in the database. This method invokes the **DeleteChallenger()** method of the **GameManager** class and returns an **HTTPApiResponse** object. It uses the **[HttpDelete]** attribute to denote that this method can be invoked only on a **DELETE** Http request, and it routes to "api/game/players/1", where "1" is the value of **ID** passed into the route table.

The following is a summary of the **GameController** API endpoints:

HTTP Method	C# Method	Endpoint (Route)	Description
GET	Get()	api/game/players	Gets all the challenger and rank data
POST	AddPlayer(Challenger user)	api/game/players	Adds a new challenger
POST	UpdateScore(Rank user)	api/game/players/score	Adds or updates a challenger score
DELETE	DeletePlayer(int id)	api/game/players/{id}	Removes a player

HTTP Method	C# Method	Endpoint (Route)	Description
GET	GetPlayerID(string email)	api/game/players/{email}	Gets the challenger ID based on e-mail
GET	GetPlayerProfile(string email)	api/game/players/profile/{email}	Gets the challenger information based on e-mail

All Web API endpoints in the example are contained within a single class, as I'm trying to make this demo as simple as possible. In a real-world scenario when you are dealing with large data models, I would strongly recommend you separate each controller implementation and follow the REST standards whenever you can. It's also recommended to always wrap your API response with meaningful results and handle possible errors. You may check out my article about writing a custom wrapper for managing API exceptions and consistent responses here for an example: `http://vmsdurano.com/asp-net-core-and-web-api-a-custom-wrapper-for-managing-exceptions-and-consistent-responses/`.

Enabling CORS

Now that we have our API endpoints ready, the final step that we are going to do on this project is to enable CORS. We need this because this API will be consumed in other applications that probably have difference domains.

Here's the CORS definition as per the documentation here: `https://msdn.microsoft.com/en-us/magazine/dn532203.aspx`

Cross-origin resource sharing (CORS) is a World Wide Web Consortium (W3C) specification (commonly considered part of HTML5) that lets JavaScript overcome the same-origin policy security restriction imposed by browsers. The same-origin policy) means that your JavaScript can only make AJAX calls back to the same origin of the containing Web page (where "origin" is defined as the combination of host name, protocol and port number). For example, JavaScript on a Web page from `http://foo.com` *can't make AJAX calls to* `http://bar.com` *(or to* `http://www.foo.com`*,* `https://foo.com` *or* `http://foo.com:999`*, for that matter).*

CORS relaxes this restriction by letting servers indicate which origins are allowed to call them. CORS is enforced by browsers but must be implemented on the server, and the most recent release of ASP.NET Web API 2 has full CORS support. With Web API 2, you can configure policy to allow JavaScript clients from a different origin to access your APIs.

To enable CORS in ASP.NET Web API, do the following:

1. Install Microsoft.AspNet.WebApi.Cors via nugget. The latest stable version as of this time of writing is 5.2.6.

2. Navigate to the **App_Start** folder and then open **WebApiConfig.cs**. Add the following code to the WebApiConfig.Register method:

   ```
   config.EnableCors();
   ```

3. Open the **GameController** class and then declare the following namespace:

   ```
   using System.Web.Http.Cors;
   ```

4. Finally, add the **[EnableCors]** attribute just like in the following:

   ```
   [EnableCors(origins: "http://localhost:60273",
   headers: "*", methods: "*")]
   public class GameController : ApiController
   ```

Note that you'll have to replace the value of origins based on the URI of the consuming client. Otherwise, you can use the "*" wildcard to allow any domain to access your API.

At this point, we are done creating the required API endpoints. Before moving into the Chapter 4, I would suggest you do a **Clean** and then **Rebuild** to ensure that the application has no compilation errors.

Sample cURLs

One of the advantages of REST APIs is that you can use almost any programming language to call the endpoint. The endpoint is simply a resource located on a web server at a specific path.

Each programming language has a different way of making web calls. Rather than exhausting your energy by trying to show how to make web calls in .NET, Java, Python, C++, JavaScript, Ruby, and so on, you can just show the call using cURL.

cURL provides a generic, language-agnostic way to demonstrate HTTP requests and responses. Users can see the format of the request, including any headers and other parameters. Your users can translate this into the specific format for the language they're using.

You can test out the API endpoints that we've created earlier yourself by using the following cURLs:

- Get All Players

```
curl -X GET \
  http://localhost:56393/api/game/players \
  -H 'Cache-Control: no-cache' \
```

- Get the Player ChallengerID

```
curl -X GET \
  http://localhost:56393/api/game/players/testemail.com/ \
  -H 'Cache-Control: no-cache' \
```

- Get the Player Profile

```
curl -X GET \
  http://localhost:56393/api/game/players/profile/
  testemail.com/ \
  -H 'Cache-Control: no-cache' \
```

- Add a New Player

```
curl -X POST \
  http://localhost:56393/api/game/players \
  -H 'Cache-Control: no-cache' \
  -H 'Content-Type: application/json' \
  -d '{
        "Email":"vynnmarkus@email.com",
        "FirstName":"Vynn Markus",
        "LastName":"Durano"
}'
```

- Update a Player Score

```
curl -X POST \
  http://localhost:56393/api/game/players/score \
  -H 'Cache-Control: no-cache' \
  -H 'Content-Type: application/json' \
  -d '{
        "ChallengerID":1,
        "Best":3,
        "DateAchieved":"9/23/2018 4:16"
}'
```

- Delete a Player

```
curl -X DELETE \
  http://localhost:56393/api/game/players/1 \
  -H 'Cache-Control: no-cache' \
```

The following table shows the cURL commands used and their descriptions from the preceding examples:

Command	Description
-X	The -X signifies the method used for the request. Common options are GET, POST, DELETE, PUT.
-H	Submits the request header to the resource. This is very common with REST API requests because the authorization is usually included in the header.
-d	Includes data to post to the URL. The data needs to be URL encoded. Data can also be passed in the request body.

For the available list of the cURL commands that you can use, see the cURL documentation here: `https://curl.haxx.se/docs/manpage.html`

Testing with Postman

You can also download Postman to test out the API endpoints that we have created earlier. Postman is really a handy tool to test APIs without needing to create a UI, and it's absolutely free. Get it here: `www.getpostman.com/`

Here's a sample screenshot of the API tested in Postman:

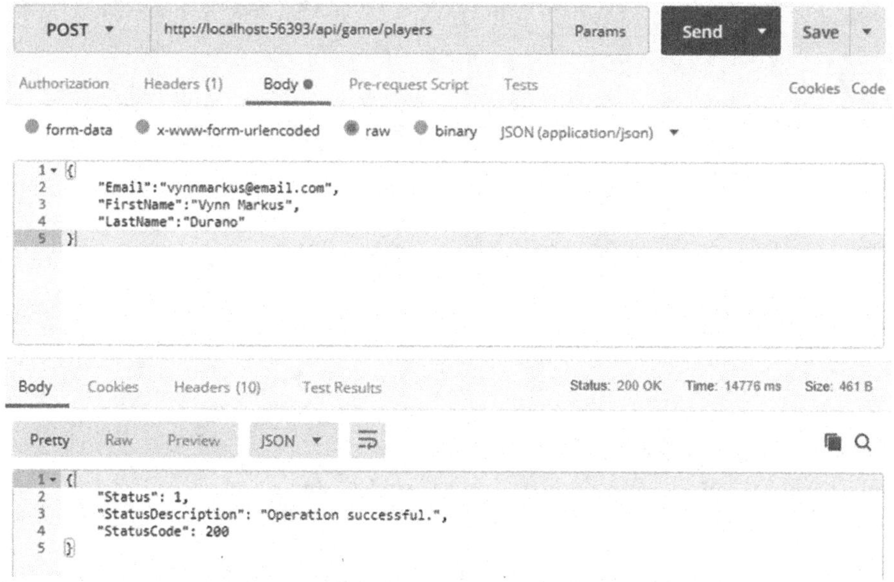

***Figure 3-11.** Testing an API with Postman*

CHAPTER 4

Building Mobile Application with Xamarin.Forms

Now that we have the API ready, we can start implementing the Memory Game mobile application and start consuming the Web API that we've just created in the Chapter 3. Go head and navigate to **MemoryGame.App** project and then create the following folders:

- **REST** – this folder is where we put the class for managing REST API calls.
- **Services** – this folder is where we put the interfaces that the application is going to need.
- **Classes** – this folder is where application-specific classes such as Helpers, Settings, and Data Manager are stored.
- **Pages** – this folder is where the XAML files needed for the application are stored.

We are doing it this way in order for us to easily manage the files by just looking at the folder for ease of navigation and maintainability.

V. M. S. Durano, *Understanding Game Application Development*,
https://doi.org/10.1007/978-1-4842-4264-3_4

Implementing the Service Interfaces

We are going to use an interface to define a common method in which other applications can implement it. This is because Android and iOS platforms have different code implementations to deal with device vibration, playing a sound, and storage.

An interface is just a skeleton of a method without the actual implementation. This means that the application which implements the interface will create a class to perform a concrete platform-specific implementation.

The IHaptic Interface

Let's create a few services that our app will need. Let's start by adding the **IHaptic** interface. To do this, right-click the **Services** folder and then select **Add ➤ New Item**. On the left pane under **Visual C# Items ➤ Code**, select **Interface** and name it "**IHaptic.cs**" just like in the following figure:

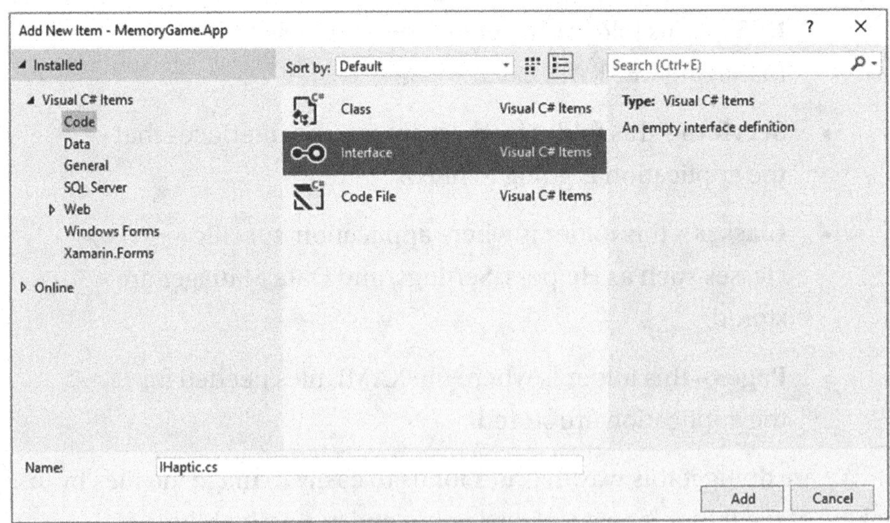

Figure 4-1. *Adding a new interface file*

Click **Add** and then replace the default generated code with the following code:

```
namespace MemoryGame.App.Services
{
    public interface IHaptic
    {
        void ActivateHaptic();
    }
}
```

The preceding code is nothing but a simple interface definition that contains a **void** method called **ActivateHaptic()**.

The ILocalDataStore Interface

Create another interface file under the **Services** folder. Name the file as "**ILocalDataSource.cs**" and replace the default generated code with the following:

```
namespace MemoryGame.App.Services
{
    public interface ILocalDataStore
    {
        void SaveSettings(string fileName, string text);
        string LoadSettings(string fileName);
    }
}
```

The **ILocalDataStore** interface contains two main methods: **SaveSettings()** takes a file name and a text as the parameter. The **LoadSettings()** method takes a file name as a parameter and returns a string type.

The ISound Interface

Lastly, create another interface and name it "**ISound.cs**". Replace the default generated code with the following:

```
namespace MemoryGame.App.Services
{
    public interface ISound
    {
        bool PlayMp3File(string fileName);
        bool PlayWavFile(string fileName);
    }
}
```

The **ISound** interface contains two main **boolean** methods: **PlayMp3File()** and **PlayWavFile(),** which takes a file name as the parameter.

The reason we are creating the preceding services/interfaces is because iOS and Android have different code implementations for setting device vibration and sound. That's why we are defining interfaces so both platforms can just inherit from it and implement code-specific logic.

Let's move on by creating the following files within the **Classes** folder:

- Helper.cs
- Settings.cs
- PlayerManager.cs
- MemoryGame.cs

The Helper Class

Create a new class called "**Helper.cs**" under the **Classes** folder and then replace the default generated code with the following code:

```
using Plugin.Connectivity;

namespace MemoryGame.App.Helper
{
    public static class StringExtensions
    {
        public static int ToInteger(this string numberString)
        {
            int result = 0;
            if (int.TryParse(numberString, out result))
                return result;
            return 0;
        }
    }

    public static class Utils
    {
        public static bool IsConnectedToInternet()
        {
            return CrossConnectivity.Current.IsConnected;
        }
    }
}
```

The **Helper.cs** file is composed of two classes: **StringExtension** and **Utils**. The **StringExtension** class contains a **ToIntenger()** extension method that accepts a **string** containing a valid numerical value and converts it into an **integer** type. The **Utils** class, on the other hand, contains an **IsConnectedToInternet()** method to verify Internet connectivity. We will be using these methods later in our application.

The Settings Class

Create another class within the **Classes** folder and name it "**Settings.cs**". Replace the default generated code with the following:

```
using Plugin.Settings;
using Plugin.Settings.Abstractions;
using System;

namespace MemoryGame.App.Classes
{
    public static class Settings
    {
        private static ISettings AppSettings => CrossSettings.
        Current;

        public static string PlayerFirstName
        {
            get => AppSettings.GetValueOrDefault(nameof(Player
            FirstName), string.Empty);
            set => AppSettings.AddOrUpdateValue(nameof(Player
            FirstName), value);
        }

        public static string PlayerLastName
        {
            get => AppSettings.GetValueOrDefault(nameof(Player
            LastName), string.Empty);
            set => AppSettings.AddOrUpdateValue(nameof(Player
            LastName), value);
        }
```

```
public static string PlayerEmail
{
    get => AppSettings.GetValueOrDefault(nameof(Player
    Email), string.Empty);
    set => AppSettings.AddOrUpdateValue(nameof(Player
    Email), value);
}

public static int TopScore
{
    get => AppSettings.GetValueOrDefault(nameof
    (TopScore), 1);
    set => AppSettings.AddOrUpdateValue(nameof
    (TopScore), value);
}

public static DateTime DateAchieved
{
    get => AppSettings.GetValueOrDefault(nameof(Date
    Achieved), DateTime.UtcNow);
    set => AppSettings.AddOrUpdateValue(nameof(Date
    Achieved), value);
}

public static bool IsProfileSync
{
    get => AppSettings.GetValueOrDefault(nameof
    (IsProfileSync), false);
    set => AppSettings.AddOrUpdateValue(nameof
    (IsProfileSync), value);
}
```

```
        public static int PlayerID
        {
            get => AppSettings.GetValueOrDefault(nameof(Player
            ID), 0);
            set => AppSettings.AddOrUpdateValue(nameof(Player
            ID), value);
        }
    }
}
```

The **Settings.cs** file contains a few static properties that we are going to use in the application. They are defined **static** so that we don't need to create an instance of the class when calling them; that's what the Helper or Utility class is meant for. We are defining them in the Settings.cs file to separate them from the Helper class for one sole purpose: having a central location for shared properties that can be accessed across all our applications. You can think of it as a local data store for the user's data and application configuration.

Let's look at a quick example:

```
public static string PlayerFirstName
{
    get => AppSettings.GetValueOrDefault(nameof(PlayerFirst
    Name), string.Empty);
    set => AppSettings.AddOrUpdateValue(nameof(PlayerFirst
    Name), value);
}
```

The **PlayerFirstName** is a **static** property that contains **Expression-Bodied Members** for getting and setting values. Expression-bodied functions are another syntax simplification in C# 6.0. These are functions with no statement body. Instead, you implement them with an expression following the function declaration.

This code is an example of expression body definition:

```
get => AppSettings.GetValueOrDefault(nameof(PlayerFirstName),
string.Empty);
```

The preceding code gets the value of **PlayerFirstName** and sets a default value to **string.Empty**.

C# 7.0 introduces this syntax for setters:

```
set => AppSettings.AddOrUpdateValue(nameof(PlayerFirstName), value);
```

The preceding code sets the **PlayerFirstName** with the new value assigned and stores it locally in the device.

For more information on Expression-Bodied Members, read the following: https://docs.microsoft.com/en-us/dotnet/csharp/programming-guide/statements-expressions-operators/expression-bodied-members

The Settings plug-in saves specific properties directly to each platform's native setting APIs (NSUserDefaults in iOS, SharedPreferences in Android, etc.). This ensures the fastest, securest, and most reliable creation and editing settings per application.

For more information about the Settings plug-in, see the following: https://jamesmontemagno.github.io/SettingsPlugin/

The DTO Class

Create another class within the **Classes** folder and name it "**DTO.cs**". Replace the default generated code with the following:

```
using System;

namespace MemoryGame.App.Classes
{
    public class PlayerProfile
    {
        public string FirstName { get; set; }
```

```
        public string LastName { get; set; }
        public string Email { get; set; }
    }

    public class PlayerScore
    {
        public int ChallengerID { get; set; }
        public byte Best { get; set; }
        public DateTime DateAchieved { get; set; }
    }

    public class PlayerData
    {
        public string FirstName { get; set; }
        public string LastName { get; set; }
        public byte Best { get; set; }
        public DateTime DateAchieved { get; set; }
    }
}
```

The DTO file contains three main classes: The **PlayerProfile**, **PlayerScore**, and **PlayerData**. We will use these classes as DTOs for passing information from one place to another.

The GameAPI Class

Since we finished creating the Web API earlier, it's time for us to create a class that consumes the API endpoints. Create a new class called "**GameAPI.cs**" under the **REST** folder and then replace the default generated code with the following code:

```
using System;
using System.Text;
using System.Threading.Tasks;
```

```
using Newtonsoft.Json;
using MemoryGame.App.Classes;
using System.Net.Http;
using System.Net.Http.Headers;

namespace MemoryGame.App.REST
{
    public class GameAPI

    {

        //replace the value of APIUri with the published URI to
        where your API is hosted.
        //E.g http://yourdomain.com/yourappname/api/game
        private const string APIUri = "http://localhost:56393/
        api/game/players";
        HttpClient client;
        public GameAPI()
        {
            client = new HttpClient();
            client.MaxResponseContentBufferSize = 256000;
            client.DefaultRequestHeaders.Clear();
            //Define request data format
            client.DefaultRequestHeaders.Accept.Add(new Media
            TypeWithQualityHeaderValue("application/json"));
        }

        public async Task<bool> SavePlayerProfile(PlayerProfile
        data, bool isNew = false)
        {
            var uri = new Uri(APIUri);

            var json = JsonConvert.SerializeObject(data);
```

```
        var content = new StringContent(json, Encoding.
        UTF8,"application/json");

        HttpResponseMessage response = null;
        if (isNew)
            response = await ProcessPostAsync(uri, content);

        if (response.IsSuccessStatusCode)
        {
            Settings.IsProfileSync = true;
            return true;
        }

        return false;
    }

    public async Task<bool> SavePlayerScore(PlayerScore data)
    {
        var uri = new Uri($"{APIUri}/score");

        var json = JsonConvert.SerializeObject(data);
        var content = new StringContent(json, Encoding.
        UTF8,"application/json");
        var response = await ProcessPostAsync(uri, content);

        if (response.IsSuccessStatusCode)
            return true;

        return false;
    }

    public async Task<int> GetPlayerID(string email)
    {
        var uri = new Uri($"{APIUri}/{email}/");
        int id = 0;
```

```
    var response = await ProcessGetAsync(uri);
    if (response.IsSuccessStatusCode)
    {
        var content = await response.Content.
        ReadAsStringAsync();
        id = JsonConvert.DeserializeObject<int>(content);
    }
    return id;
}

public async Task<PlayerData> GetPlayerData(string
email)
{
    var uri = new Uri($"{APIUri}/profile/{email}/");
    PlayerData player = null;

    var response = await ProcessGetAsync(uri);
    if (response.IsSuccessStatusCode)
    {
        player = new PlayerData();
        var content = await response.Content.
        ReadAsStringAsync();
        player = JsonConvert.DeserializeObject
        <PlayerData>(content);
    }

    return player;
}

private async Task<HttpResponseMessage>
ProcessPostAsync(Uri uri, StringContent content)
{
    return await client.PostAsync(uri, content);
}
```

```
        private async Task<HttpResponseMessage>
        ProcessGetAsync(Uri uri)
        {
            return await client.GetAsync(uri);
        }
    }
}
```

The preceding code is pretty much self-explanatory, as you could probably guess by its method name. The class just contains a method that calls the API endpoints that we created in the previous section. If the code does not make sense to you now, don't worry as we will talk about it later in this section.

Async and Await Overview

Before we dig into the code implementation details of the **GameAPI** class, let's have a quick overview of the **Async** and **Await** concepts in C#.

Asynchronous programming is all about writing code that allows several things to happen at the same time without "blocking," or waiting for other things to complete. This is different from synchronous programming, in which everything happens in the order it is written. In order to perform an asynchronous operation, a method should be marked as **async:** this tells the compiler that the method can run asynchronously. The **await** keyword is used in conjunction with the async keyword to tell the compiler to wait for the **Task** without blocking code execution.

The **async** keyword only enables the **await** keyword. The **await** keyword is where things can get asynchronous. Await is like a unary operator: it takes a single argument, an awaitable **Task** or **Task<T>** (an "awaitable" is an asynchronous operation). Await examines that awaitable to see if it has already completed; if the awaitable has already completed, then the method just continues running (synchronously, just like a regular method).

The **Task** and **Task<T>** represent an asynchronous operation that can be waited. A **Task** does not return a value, while **Task<T>** does.

Note If an async method doesn't use an await operator to mark a suspension point, the method executes as a synchronous method does, despite the async modifier. The compiler issues a warning for such methods.

Here's a brief definition of the async and await keywords taken from the official documentation here: `https://docs.microsoft.com/en-us/dotnet/csharp/programming-guide/concepts/async/`

The async and await keywords in C# are the heart of async programming. By using those two keywords, you can use resources in the .NET Framework, .NET Core, or the Windows Runtime to create an asynchronous method almost as easily as you create a synchronous method. Asynchronous methods that you define by using the async keyword are referred to as async methods.

Method Definitions

Now that you have a basic idea regarding how asynchronous programming works, let's see what the code does by breaking them. Let's start with the **GameAPI** constructor code block:

```
private const string APIUri = "http://localhost:56393/api/game/
players";
HttpClient client;
public GameAPI()
{
    client = new HttpClient();
    client.MaxResponseContentBufferSize = 256000;
```

```
    client.DefaultRequestHeaders.Clear();
    //Define request data format
    client.DefaultRequestHeaders.Accept.Add(new MediaTypeWith
    QualityHeaderValue("application/json"));
}
```

The **APIUri** is a **private** variable that holds the base API endpoint value. In this example, it uses the value `http://localhost:56393/api/game/players`, which points to my local development IIS Express host. The value "`http://localhost:56393`" is automatically created for you once you run the application in Visual Studio. You need to change this value with the published URI to where your API is hosted. We'll talk more about that later in the Chapter 6.

It was my intent to put the value of APIUri within the GameAPI class for the sake of simplicity. In real-world applications, it is recommended to store the value of APIUri in a configuration file, where you can easily modify the value.

The **HttpClient** object is declared on the second line. HttpClient is a modern HTTP client for .NET. It provides a flexible and extensible API for accessing all things exposed through HTTP.

On the next line is the **GameAPI** class constructor. This is where the HttpClient is initialized and configured with a few properties for setting the **MaxResponseContentBufferSize** and **DefaultRequestHeader** media type.

Next code block:

```
public async Task<bool> SavePlayerProfile(PlayerProfile data,
bool isNew = false)
{
    var uri = new Uri(APIUri);

    var json = JsonConvert.SerializeObject(data);
    var content = new StringContent(json, Encoding.UTF8,"
    application/json");
```

```
    HttpResponseMessage response = null;
    if (isNew)
        response = await ProcessPostAsync(uri, content);

    if (response.IsSuccessStatusCode)
    {
        Settings.IsProfileSync = true;
        return true;
    }

    return false;
}
```

The **SavePlayerProfile()** takes a **PlayerProfile** object and an optional **bool isNew** flag parameter. This method is defined as asynchronous by marking it as **async** and returns a **Task** of type **bool**.

Inside the method, we define a new **Uri** object that takes the **APIUri** as the parameter. We then serialize the data using Newtonsoft's **JsonCovert.SerializeObject()** method and pass the result into a **json** variable. After the data has been serialized, we create a StringContent object with the format "application/json" and the encoding set to UTF8. The **StringContent** class creates a formatted text appropriate for the http server/client communication. After a client request, a server will respond with an **HttpResponseMessage** and that response will need a content; that can be created with the **StringContent** class.

In the next line, we create an instance of the **HttpResponseMessage** object and we check for the **isNew** flag to do some validation. If the flag value is **true**, we call an awaitable **Task** called **ProcessPostAsync()** and pass along the **uri** and **content** values. The awaitable **Task** return is then assigned to an **HttpResponseMessage** object called **response**. If the response is successful, then we set the value of **Settings.IsProfileSync** to **true** and return **true** to the method. Otherwise, if the flag value is **false** or the response isn't successful, we simply return **false** to the method.

Next code block:

```
public async Task<bool> SavePlayerScore(PlayerScore data)
{
    var uri = new Uri($"{APIUri}/score");

    var json = JsonConvert.SerializeObject(data);
    var content = new StringContent(json, Encoding.UTF8,
    "application/json");
    var response = await ProcessPostAsync(uri, content);

    if (response.IsSuccessStatusCode)
        return true;

    return false;
}
```

The **SavePlayerScore()** method is also an asynchronous method that takes a **PlayerScore** object as a parameter. The first line in the method defines a new **Uri** object that takes the **$"{APIUri}/score"** as the parameter. The **$** character denotes an **interpolated string**. You can think of it as a shorthand syntax for the **string.Format** method, but it's more readable and convenient. In this case, the value of *$"{APIUri}/score"* will be translated to *"http://localhost:56393/api/game/players/score"*.

Next, we serialize the data using Newtonsoft's **JsonCovert. SerializeObject()** method and pass the result into a **json** variable. After the data has been serialized, we then create a **StringContent** object with specific formatting. It then returns **true** for a successful response and otherwise returns **false**.

Next code block:

```
public async Task<int> GetPlayerID(string email)
{
    var uri = new Uri($"{APIUri}/{email}/");
    int id = 0;
```

```
    var response = await ProcessGetAsync(uri);
    if (response.IsSuccessStatusCode)
    {
        var content = await response.Content.
        ReadAsStringAsync();
        id = JsonConvert.DeserializeObject<int>(content);
    }

    return id;
}
```

The **GetPlayerID()** method is an asynchronous method that takes a **string** as a parameter and returns a **Task** of type **int**. Just like the previous async methods, the first line defines a new **Uri** object that takes an interpolated string value. The *$"{APIUri}/{email}/"* will be translated to something like *"http://localhost:56393/api/game/players/testemail.com/"*.

The next line initializes a variable called **id** of type **int** with a default value of **0**. It then calls an awaitable **Task** called **ProcessGetAsync()**and passes the **uri** variable to it. If the response is successful, it calls another awaitable **Task** called **ReadAsStringAsync()** and assigns the result to a variable called **content**. It then deserializes the **content** value using Newtonsoft's **JsonConvert.DeserializeObject()** and assigns the result to the variable called **id**. Finally, the value of **id** is returned to the method.

Next code block:

```
public async Task<PlayerData> GetPlayerData(string email)
{
    var uri = new Uri($"{APIUri}/profile/{email}/");
    PlayerData player = null;
```

```
    var response = await ProcessGetAsync(uri);
    if (response.IsSuccessStatusCode)
    {
        player = new PlayerData();
        var content = await response.Content.
        ReadAsStringAsync();
        player = JsonConvert.DeserializeObject<PlayerData>
        (content);
    }

    return player;
}
```

The preceding method is pretty much similar to the **GetPlayerID()** method except that it returns an **object** rather than an **int**. The **GetPlayerData()** method is also an asynchronous method that takes a **string** as a parameter and returns a **Task** of type **PlayerData**. The **PlayerData** is a class we defined in the **DTO** file that houses a few properties. The first line within the method defines a new **Uri** object that takes an interpolated string value. The *$"{APIUri}/profile/{email}/"* value will be translated to something like *"http://localhost:56393/api/game/players/profile/testemail.com/"*.

The next line initializes a variable called **player** of type **PlayerData**. It then calls an awaitable **Task** called **ProcessGetAsync()** and passes the **uri** variable to it. If the response is successful, it calls another awaitable **Task** called **ReadAsStringAsync()** and assigns the result to a variable called **content**. It then deserializes the **content** value using Newtonsoft's **JsonConvert.DeserializeObject()** and assigns the result to the variable called **player**. If the response is not successful, then it returns the **player** variable with a **null** value to the method; otherwise, it returns the **player** variable with the associated data assigned from the API response.

Next code block:

```
private async Task<HttpResponseMessage> ProcessPostAsync(Uri
uri, StringContent content)
{
    return await client.PostAsync(uri, content); ;
}

private async Task<HttpResponseMessage> ProcessGetAsync(Uri uri)
{
    return await client.GetAsync(uri);
}
```

The last two private methods in the preceding are used to handle common operations. The **ProcessPostAsync()** is an async method that takes a **Uri** and **StringContent** as parameters and returns a **Task** of type **HttpResponseMessage.** This method basically calls the **PostAsync()** method of the **HttpClient** object.

On the other hand, the **ProcessGetAsync()** takes only a **Uri** as a parameter and returns a **Task** of type **HttpResponseMessage.** This method calls the **GetAsync()** method of the **HttpClient** object.

For more information on consuming Web API from a .NET client, see the following: https://docs.microsoft.com/en-us/aspnet/web-api/overview/advanced/calling-a-web-api-from-a-net-client

The PlayerManager Class

Now let's create the class for managing the player data and score. Create a new class under the **Classes** folder and name it "**PlayerManager.cs**" and then copy the following code:

```
using MemoryGame.App.Helper;
using System;
using System.Threading.Tasks;
```

```
namespace MemoryGame.App.Classes
{
    public static class PlayerManager
    {
        public static void Save(PlayerProfile player)
        {
            Settings.PlayerFirstName = player.FirstName;
            Settings.PlayerLastName = player.LastName;
            Settings.PlayerEmail = player.Email;
        }

        public static PlayerProfile GetPlayerProfileFromLocal()
        {
            return new PlayerProfile
            {
                FirstName = Settings.PlayerFirstName,
                LastName = Settings.PlayerLastName,
                Email = Settings.PlayerEmail
            };
        }

        public static PlayerScore GetPlayerScoreFromLocal()
        {
            return new PlayerScore
            {
                ChallengerID = Settings.PlayerID,
                Best = Convert.ToByte(Settings.TopScore),
                DateAchieved = Settings.DateAchieved
            };
        }
```

```
public static void UpdateBest(int score)
{
    if (Settings.TopScore < score)
    {
        Settings.TopScore = score;
        Settings.DateAchieved = DateTime.UtcNow;
    }
}

public static int GetBestScore(int currentLevel)
{
    if (Settings.TopScore > currentLevel)
        return Settings.TopScore;
    else
        return currentLevel;
}

public async static Task<bool> Sync()
{
    REST.GameAPI api = new REST.GameAPI();
    bool result = false;

    try
    {
        if (!Settings.IsProfileSync)
            result = await api.SavePlayerProfile(Player
            Manager.GetPlayerProfileFromLocal(), true);

        if (Settings.PlayerID == 0)
            Settings.PlayerID = await api.GetPlayerID
            (Settings.PlayerEmail);

        result = await api.SavePlayerScore(PlayerManager.
        GetPlayerScoreFromLocal());
```

```
            }
            catch
            {
                return result;
            }
        return result;
    }

    public async static Task<bool> CheckScoreAndSync(int score)
    {
        if (Settings.TopScore < score)
        {
            UpdateBest(score);
            if (Utils.IsConnectedToInternet())
            {
                var response = await Sync();
                return response == true ? true : false;
            }
            else
                return false;
        }
        else
            return false;
    }

    public async static Task<PlayerData> CheckExistingPlayer
    (string email)
    {
        REST.GameAPI api = new REST.GameAPI();
        PlayerData player = new PlayerData();
        if (Utils.IsConnectedToInternet())
```

```
            {
                player = await api.GetPlayerData(email);
            }

            return player;
        }
    }
}
```

The **PlayerManager** class is composed of a few methods for handling data retrieval and syncing. The class and methods are marked with the keyword **static,** so we can directly reference them without instantiating the object. Since this class is not tied up to any object that can change the behavior of the class itself and its member, it makes more sense to use static. Notice that each method calls the method defined in the **GameAPI** class. We did it like this so we can separate the actual code logic for ease of maintenance and separation of concerns.

Let's take a look at what we did there by breaking the code into sections. Let's start with the **Save()** method:

```
public static void Save(PlayerProfile player)
{
    Settings.PlayerFirstName = player.FirstName;
    Settings.PlayerLastName = player.LastName;
    Settings.PlayerEmail = player.Email;
}
```

The **Save()** method takes a **PlayerProfile** object as a parameter. The **PlayerProfile** is an object that we define in the **DTO** file, which houses a few properties. The code basically stores the value from the **PlayerProfile** object properties to the **Settings** properties. In other words, this method saves the player profile such as FirstName, LastName, and Email in the device's local storage for future use.

Next code block:

```
public static PlayerProfile GetPlayerProfileFromLocal()
{
    return new PlayerProfile
    {
        FirstName = Settings.PlayerFirstName,
        LastName = Settings.PlayerLastName,
        Email = Settings.PlayerEmail
    };
}
```

The **GetPlayerProfileFromLocal()** method is the opposite of the **Save()** method. The code fetches the player information from the local device data storage and assigns them to the **PlayerProfile** object.

Next code block:

```
public static void UpdateBest(int score)
{
    if (Settings.TopScore < score)
    {
        Settings.TopScore = score;
        Settings.DateAchieved = DateTime.UtcNow;
    }
}
```

As the method name suggests, the **UpdateBest()** method updates the challenger score. The code checks for the existing top score from the local data store and updates the **TopScore** property with the current score if the challenger score is greater than the existing top score.

Next code block:

```
public static int GetBestScore(int currentLevel)
{
    if (Settings.TopScore > currentLevel)
        return Settings.TopScore;
    else
        return currentLevel;
}
```

The **GetBestScore()** method takes an int as a parameter. The code basically compares the current score/level with the score from the local data storage and returns the highest value.

Next code block:

```
public async static Task<bool> Sync()
{
    REST.GameAPI api = new REST.GameAPI();
    bool result = false;

    try
    {
        if (!Settings.IsProfileSync)
            result = await api.SavePlayerProfile(PlayerManager.
            GetPlayerProfileFromLocal(), true);
        if (Settings.PlayerID == 0)
            Settings.PlayerID = await api.GetPlayerID(Settings.
            PlayerEmail);

        result = await api.SavePlayerScore(PlayerManager.
        GetPlayerScoreFromLocal());
    }
```

```
    catch
    {
        return result;
    }

    return result;
}
```

The **Sync()** method is an asynchronous method that returns a **Task** of type **bool**. The first line creates an instance of the **GameApi** object. If you remember, the **GameApi** class contains the code for communicating with the Web API endpoints. The next line of code initializes a **bool** flag in a variable called **result**.

Within **try-block**, the code checks if the challenger profile is already synced. If not, then it calls an awaitable **Task** from the **GameApi** class called **SavePlayerProfile(),** which takes a **PlayerProfile** object as the parameter and a **bool** parameter that indicates if the profile is new. The next **if-condition** checks for the existence of the challenger profile by validating the **PlayerID** property, which is stored in the local data storage. If the value is 0, then it calls an awaitable **Task** called **GetPlayerID(),** with an e-mail as the parameter, and assigns the result back to the **Settings. PlayerID** property. Otherwise, if the challenger already did a sync, it just updates the challenger score by calling the **SavePlayerScore()** Task.

If the code within the **try-block** fails, then it should go to the **catch-block** and return a **false** value to the method, indicating that the sync wasn't successful.

Note In real-world applications, it is recommended to handle specific exceptions and log them for debugging and easy troubleshooting.

Next code block:

```
public async static Task<bool> CheckScoreAndSync(int score)
{
    if (Settings.TopScore < score)
    {
        UpdateBest(score);
        if (Utils.IsConnectedToInternet())
        {
            var response = await Sync();
            return response == true ? true : false;
        }
        else
            return false;
    }
    else
        return false;
}
```

The **CheckScoreAndSync()** is also an asynchronous method that takes an **int** as a parameter and returns a **Task** of type **bool**. The code basically validates the score; if the current score is greater than the existing top score, then it updates the existing top score from the local data storage with the current score and ultimately calls the **Sync()** method.

Next code block:

```
public async static Task<PlayerData> CheckExistingPlayer(string
email)
{
    REST.GameAPI api = new REST.GameAPI();
    PlayerData player = new PlayerData();
```

```
    if (Utils.IsConnectedToInternet())
    {
        player = await api.GetPlayerData(email);
    }

    return player;
}
```

The **CheckExistingPlayer()** is an asynchronous method that takes a string as a parameter and returns a **Task** of type **PlayerData**. This method simply calls the awaitable **Task** called **GetPlayerData()** from the GameApi class and takes an e-mail as the parameter.

Here's a quick definition of each of these methods:

- The **Save()** method saves the player information in the local device storage using the Settings plug-in.
- The **GetPlayerProfileFromLocal()** method fetches the player information from the local device storage.
- The **GetPlayerScoreFromLocal()** method fetches the player score details from the local device storage.
- The **UpdateBest()** method updates the player score in the local device storage.
- The **GetBestScore()** method fetches the player top score from the local device storage.
- The asynchronous **Sync()** method syncs the player profile and score details with data from the database into the local data storage.
- The asynchronous **CheckScoreAndSync()** method updates the top score to the database.
- The asynchronous **CheckExistingPlayer()** method verifies the existence of a challenger from the database.

Adding the Needed Graphics and Sound File

Go ahead and download the images and file sound at the following links:

- Graphics: `https://github.com/proudmonkey/Xamarin.MemoryGameApp/tree/master/MemoryGame.App/MemoryGame.App.Droid/Resources/drawable`
- Sound: `https://github.com/proudmonkey/Xamarin.MemoryGameApp/tree/master/MemoryGame.App/MemoryGame.App.Droid/Resources/raw`

Android

For Xamarin.Android, add the required images under the "**Resources/drawable**" folder. Right-click the **drawable** folder and then select **Add ➤ Existing** Item. Locate the images that you have just downloaded from the previous step and then click **Add**. The drawable folder should look like something in the following figure:

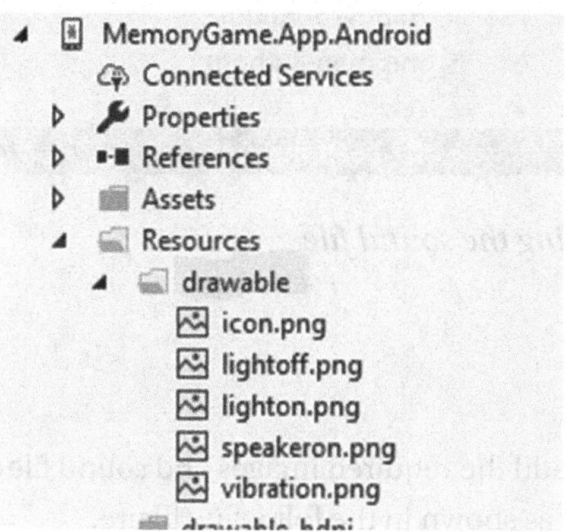

Figure 4-2. *Adding the graphics file*

To add the sound file, we need to create the "**raw**" folder first. Now go ahead and add a new folder under the **Resources** folder and name it "**raw**". Add the beep.mp3 file within the folder just like in the following figure:

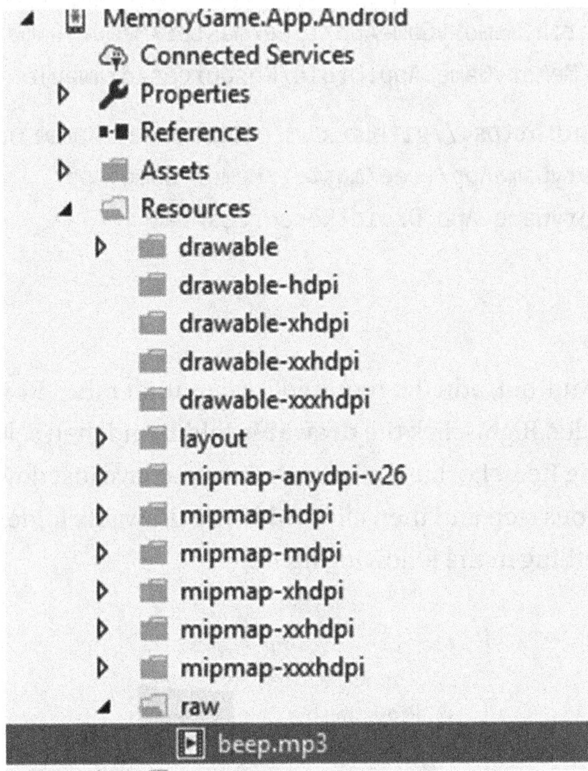

Figure 4-3. *Adding the sound file*

iOS

For Xamarin.iOS, add the required images and sound file under the "**Resource**" folder as shown in the following figure.

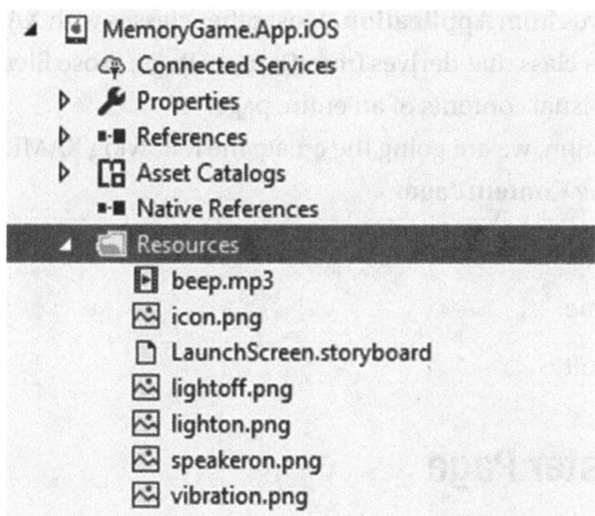

Figure 4-4. *Adding the graphics and sound files*

The Required XAML Pages

Before starting to create the required pages for the application, let's talk a bit about the anatomy of the XAML file. When we created the **MemogyGame.App** project, a pair of files are automatically with the following names:

- App.xaml, the XAML file; and
- App.xaml.cs, a C# code-behind file associated with the XAML file.

If you are working with ASP.NET WebForms, you will notice that the concept of the XAML file is pretty much the same as that of the WebForm's ASPX files. You'll need to click the arrow next to App.xaml to see the code-behind file. Both **App.xaml** and **App.xaml.cs** contribute to a class named

App that derives from **Application**. Most other classes with XAML files contribute to a class that derives from **ContentPage**; those files use XAML to define the visual contents of an entire page.

In this section, we are going the create the following XAML files that derive from the **ContentPage**.

- Register
- Home
- Result

The Register Page

Let's start building the Register page. Right-click the **Pages** folder and then select **Add ➤ New Item**. On the left pane under **Visual C# Items ➤ Xamarin.Forms**, select **Content Page** just like in the following figure:

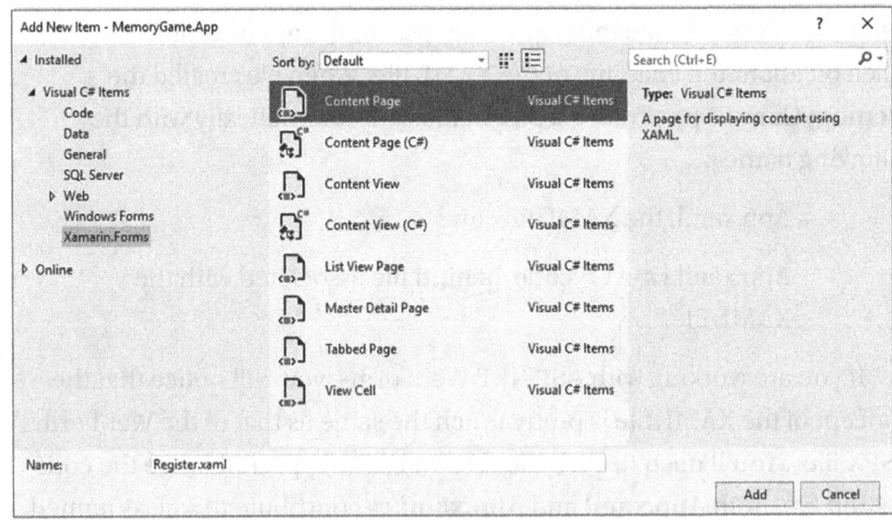

***Figure 4-5.** Creating a new ContentPage file*

Name the page "**Register**" and click **Add**.

Replace the default generated markup with the following:

```
<?xml version="1.0" encoding="utf-8" ?>
<ContentPage xmlns="http://xamarin.com/schemas/2014/forms"
             xmlns:x="http://schemas.microsoft.com/winfx/2009/
             xaml"
             x:Class="MemoryGame.App.Pages.Register">

    <StackLayout VerticalOptions="CenterAndExpand">
        <Label Text="Working Memory Game"
               FontSize="Large"
               HorizontalOptions="Center"
               VerticalOptions="CenterAndExpand" />

        <Label x:Name="lblWelcome"
               Text="Register to start the fun, or Log-on to
               continue the challenge!"
               FontSize="Small"
               HorizontalOptions="Center"
               VerticalOptions="CenterAndExpand" />

        <StackLayout x:Name="layoutChoose"
                     Orientation="Horizontal"
                     Spacing="5"
                     VerticalOptions="CenterAndExpand"
                     HorizontalOptions="Center">

            <Button x:Name="btnNew"
                    Text="Register"
                    FontSize="Medium"
                    HorizontalOptions="Center"
                    VerticalOptions="CenterAndExpand"
                    Clicked="OnbtnNewClicked"/>
```

```
        <Button x:Name="btnReturn"
                Text="Log-on"
                FontSize="Medium"
                HorizontalOptions="Center"
                VerticalOptions="CenterAndExpand"
                Clicked="OnbtnReturnClicked"/>.
</StackLayout>

<StackLayout x:Name="layoutRegister"
             VerticalOptions="CenterAndExpand"
             IsVisible="False">

        <Label Text="First Name" />
        <Entry x:Name="entryFirstName" />
        <Label Text="Last Name" />
        <Entry x:Name="entryLastName" />
        <Label Text="Email" />
        <Entry x:Name="entryEmail" />

        <StackLayout Orientation="Horizontal"
                     Spacing="3"
                     HorizontalOptions="Center">

               <Button x:Name="btnRegister"
                       Text="Let's Do This!"
                       HorizontalOptions="Center"
                       VerticalOptions="CenterAndExpand"
                       Clicked="OnbtnRegisterClicked"/>

               <Button x:Name="btnCancelRegister"
                       Text="Cancel"
                       HorizontalOptions="Center"
                       VerticalOptions="CenterAndExpand"
                       Clicked="OnbtnCancelRegister
                       Clicked"/>
```

```
            </StackLayout>
        </StackLayout>

        <StackLayout x:Name="layoutLogin"
                     VerticalOptions="CenterAndExpand"
                     IsVisible="False">

            <Label Text="Email" />
            <Entry x:Name="entryExistingEmail" />

            <StackLayout Orientation="Horizontal" Spacing="3"
            HorizontalOptions="Center">

                <Button x:Name="btnLogin"
                        Text="Let me in!"
                        HorizontalOptions="Center"
                        VerticalOptions="CenterAndExpand"
                        Clicked="OnbtnLoginClicked"/>

                <Button x:Name="btnCancelLogin"
                        Text="Cancel"
                        HorizontalOptions="Center"
                        VerticalOptions="CenterAndExpand"
                        Clicked="OnbtnCancelLoginClicked"/>

            </StackLayout>

        </StackLayout>
    </StackLayout>
</ContentPage>
```

The preceding markup uses XAML to build the application UI. XAML allows you to define UIs in Xamarin.Forms applications using markup rather than code. You may have noticed that it contains some **StackLayout** elements to group controls in certain areas in the form. The controls are used to present the form to UI and are referred to as **Button**, **Entry**, **Label**, and more. Each button from the preceding markup has a **Clicked** event attached to it to perform a certain action in the server (a.k.a. code-behind).

For comprehensive documentation about XAML in Xamarin. Forms, see the following: https://docs.microsoft.com/en-us/xamarin/xamarin-forms/xaml/xaml-basics/

Now open the **Register.xaml.cs** file and replace the default generated code with the following code:

```
using MemoryGame.App.Classes;
using MemoryGame.App.Helper;
using System;
using System.Threading.Tasks;
using Xamarin.Forms;
using Xamarin.Forms.Xaml;

namespace MemoryGame.App.Pages
{
    [XamlCompilation(XamlCompilationOptions.Compile)]
       public partial class Register : ContentPage
       {
             public Register ()
             {
                   InitializeComponent ();
             }

        enum EntryOption
        {
            Register = 0,
            Returning = 1,
            Cancel = 2
        }
```

```
protected override void OnAppearing()
{
    base.OnAppearing();
    NavigationPage.SetHasBackButton(this, false);

    if (!string.IsNullOrEmpty(Settings.PlayerFirstName))
        App._navPage.PushAsync(App._homePage);
}

async Task CheckExistingProfileAndSave(string email)
{
     try
     {
          PlayerData player = await PlayerManager.
          CheckExistingPlayer(email);
          if (string.IsNullOrEmpty(player.FirstName) &&
          string.IsNullOrEmpty(player.LastName))
          {
              await App.Current.MainPage.DisplayAlert
              ("Error", "Email does not exist.", "OK");
          }
          else
          {
              Settings.PlayerFirstName = player.
              FirstName.Trim();
              Settings.PlayerLastName = player.
              LastName.Trim();
              Settings.PlayerEmail = email.Trim();
              Settings.TopScore = player.Best;
              Settings.DateAchieved = player.DateAchieved;

          await App._navPage.PushAsync(App._homePage);
          }
     }
```

```
        catch
        {
            await App.Current.MainPage.DisplayAlert("Oops",
            "An error occurred while connecting to the
            server. Please check your connection.", "OK");
        }
    }

    async Task Save()
    {
        Settings.PlayerFirstName=entryFirstName.Text.Trim();
        Settings.PlayerLastName = entryLastName.Text.Trim();
        Settings.PlayerEmail = entryEmail.Text.Trim();

        await App._navPage.PushAsync(App._homePage);
    }

    void ToggleEntryView(EntryOption option)
    {
        switch (option)
        {
            case EntryOption.Register:
               {
                  lblWelcome.IsVisible = false;
                  layoutChoose.IsVisible = false;
                  layoutLogin.IsVisible = false;
                  layoutRegister.IsVisible = true;
                  break;
               }
            case EntryOption.Returning:
               {
                   lblWelcome.IsVisible = false;
                   layoutChoose.IsVisible = false;
                   layoutRegister.IsVisible = false;
```

```
                layoutLogin.IsVisible = true;
                break;
                }
            case EntryOption.Cancel:
                {
                     lblWelcome.IsVisible = true;
                      layoutChoose.IsVisible = true;
                      layoutRegister.IsVisible = false;
                      layoutLogin.IsVisible = false;
                      break;
                }
        }
}

void OnbtnNewClicked(object sender, EventArgs args)
{
        ToggleEntryView(EntryOption.Register);
}

void OnbtnReturnClicked(object sender, EventArgs args)
{
        ToggleEntryView(EntryOption.Returning);
}

void OnbtnCancelLoginClicked(object sender, EventArgs args)
{
        ToggleEntryView(EntryOption.Cancel);
}

void OnbtnCancelRegisterClicked(object sender, EventArgs
args)
{
        ToggleEntryView(EntryOption.Cancel);
}
```

```
async void OnbtnRegisterClicked(object sender, EventArgs args)
{
     btnRegister.IsEnabled = false;

     if (string.IsNullOrEmpty(entryFirstName.Text)
         || string.IsNullOrEmpty(entryLastName.Text)
         || string.IsNullOrEmpty(entryEmail.Text))
         await App.Current.MainPage.
         DisplayAlert("Error", "Please supply the
         required fields.", "Got it");
     else
        await Save();

     btnRegister.IsEnabled = true;
 }

async void OnbtnLoginClicked(object sender, EventArgs args)
{
     if (string.IsNullOrEmpty(entryExistingEmail.Text))
         await App.Current.MainPage.DisplayAlert("Error",
         "Please supply your email.", "Got it");
     else
     {
         if (Utils.IsConnectedToInternet())
         {
             btnLogin.IsEnabled = false;
             await CheckExistingProfileAndSave
             (entryExistingEmail.Text);
         }
         else
         {
             await App.Current.MainPage.
             DisplayAlert("Error", "No internet
             connection.", "OK");
```

```
                }
            }

            btnLogin.IsEnabled = true;
        }
    }
}
```

Let's take a look at the code implementation details by breaking them into sections. Let's start with this:

```
using MemoryGame.App.Classes;
using MemoryGame.App.Helper;
using System;
using System.Threading.Tasks;
using Xamarin.Forms;
using Xamarin.Forms.Xaml;
```

At the very top, you'll find a series of **using** keywords. This type of keyword is typically used as a directive, when it is used to create an alias for a namespace or to import types defined in other namespaces. In other words, when you want to access a certain class in your code, you need to define the namespace first.

Next code block:

```
[XamlCompilation(XamlCompilationOptions.Compile)]
public partial class Register : ContentPage
{
    public Register()
    {
        InitializeComponent();
    }
}
```

The **Register** class is a **partial** class that derives from a **ContentPage** class. In XAML, a ContentPage is a page that displays a single View, often a container like a StackLayout or ScrollView. Within the class constructor, it calls the method **InitializeComponent()**, which initializes a new **ContentPage** instance.

Next code block:

```
enumEntryOption
{
    Register = 0,
    Returning = 1,
    Cancel = 2
}
```

The preceding code is an enumeration used for toggling the buttons on the page.

Next code block:

```
protected override void OnAppearing()
{
    base.OnAppearing();
    NavigationPage.SetHasBackButton(this, false);

    if (!string.IsNullOrEmpty(Settings.PlayerFirstName))
        App._navPage.PushAsync(App._homePage);
}
```

The **OnAppearing()** is a built-in event of a page. This event is marked as **virtual**, meaning that we can override this event to customize the behavior immediately prior to the page becoming visible. In this case, we call the **SetHasBackButton()** method to hide the back button navigation when the **Register** page is loaded. The if-condition line checks the existence of the challenger's name. If the property PlayerFirstName has a value, then it redirects the view to the **Home** page; otherwise, it stays in the **Register** page.

For more information about Xamarin.Forms navigation, see the following: https://docs.microsoft.com/en-us/xamarin/xamarin-forms/app-fundamentals/navigation/

Next code block:

```
async Task CheckExistingProfileAndSave(string email)
{
    try
    {
        PlayerData player = await PlayerManager.Check
        ExistingPlayer(email);
        if (string.IsNullOrEmpty(player.FirstName) && string.
        IsNullOrEmpty(player.LastName))
        {
            await App.Current.MainPage.DisplayAlert("Error",
            "Email does not exist.", "OK");
        }
        else
        {
            Settings.PlayerFirstName = player.FirstName.Trim();
            Settings.PlayerLastName = player.LastName.Trim();
            Settings.PlayerEmail = email.Trim();
            Settings.TopScore = player.Best;
            Settings.DateAchieved = player.DateAchieved;

            await App._navPage.PushAsync(App._homePage);
        }
    }
    catch
    {
        await App.Current.MainPage.DisplayAlert("Oops", "An
        error occurred while connecting to the server. Please
        check your connection.", "OK");
    }
}
```

The **CheckExistingProfileAndSave()** is an asynchronous method that takes a **string** as the parameter and returns a **Task**. The first line within the try-block calls the awaitable **Task** called **CheckExistingPlayer()** and assigns the result to a type of **PlayerData**. If the **FirstName** and **LastName** of the **PlayerData** object are null or empty, then it displays an error stating that the e-mail provided does not exist. Otherwise, it stores the challenger information in the local data storage via **Settings** properties.

Next code block:

```
async Task Save()
{
    Settings.PlayerFirstName = entryFirstName.Text.Trim();
    Settings.PlayerLastName = entryLastName.Text.Trim();
    Settings.PlayerEmail = entryEmail.Text.Trim();

    await App._navPage.PushAsync(App._homePage);
}
```

The **Save()** method stores the basic challenger information such as **FirstName**, **LastName**, and **Email** and then automatically redirects to the **Home** page.

Next code block:

```
void ToggleEntryView(EntryOption option)
{
    switch (option)
    {
        case EntryOption.Register:
            {
                lblWelcome.IsVisible = false;
                layoutChoose.IsVisible = false;
                layoutLogin.IsVisible = false;
                layoutRegister.IsVisible = true;
                break;
            }
```

```
        case EntryOption.Returning:
            {
                lblWelcome.IsVisible = false;
                layoutChoose.IsVisible = false;
                layoutRegister.IsVisible = false;
                layoutLogin.IsVisible = true;
                break;
            }
        case EntryOption.Cancel:
            {
                lblWelcome.IsVisible = true;
                layoutChoose.IsVisible = true;
                layoutRegister.IsVisible = false;
                layoutLogin.IsVisible = false;
                break;
            }
    }
}
```

The **ToggleEntryView()** method takes an **EntryOption** enumeration as a parameter. This method basically handles the switching of register and login container layout in the **Register** page.

Next code block:

```
void OnbtnNewClicked(object sender, EventArgs args)
{
    ToggleEntryView(EntryOption.Register);
}

void OnbtnReturnClicked(object sender, EventArgs args)
{
    ToggleEntryView(EntryOption.Returning);
}
```

```
void OnbtnCancelLoginClicked(object sender, EventArgs args)
{
    ToggleEntryView(EntryOption.Cancel);
}

void OnbtnCancelRegisterClicked(object sender, EventArgs args)
{
    ToggleEntryView(EntryOption.Cancel);
}
```

The preceding code comprises event handlers for buttons that invoke the **ToggleEntryView()** method. The **OnbtnNewClicked** event shows the **Register** view with a cancel button. The **OnbtnReturnClicked** event, on the other hand, shows the **Login** view with a cancel button. The remaining events are used to revert the view to original state.

Next code block:

```
async void OnbtnRegisterClicked(object sender, EventArgs args)
{
    btnRegister.IsEnabled = false;

    if (string.IsNullOrEmpty(entryFirstName.Text)
        || string.IsNullOrEmpty(entryLastName.Text)
        || string.IsNullOrEmpty(entryEmail.Text))
        await App.Current.MainPage.DisplayAlert("Error",
        "Please supply the required fields.", "Got it");
    else
        await Save();

    btnRegister.IsEnabled = true;
}
```

The **OnbtnRegisterClicked** is an asynchronous event that returns **void**. As you may know, **async** methods can return **Task<T>**, **Task**, or **void**. In almost all cases, you want to return **Task<T>** or **Task**, and return

void only when you have to. Returning **void** for **async event handlers** is great, as we can perform asynchronous operations without blocking the UI thread.

The first line of the code within the event disables the button **btnRegister** and then performs some asynchronous operations. If the **FirstName**, **LastName**, and **Email** fields are left empty, then it shows an error. Otherwise, it calls the **Save()** method.

Next code block:

```
async void OnbtnLoginClicked(object sender, EventArgs args)
{
    if (string.IsNullOrEmpty(entryExistingEmail.Text))
        await App.Current.MainPage.DisplayAlert("Error",
        "Please supply your email.", "Got it");
    else
    {
        if (Utils.IsConnectedToInternet())
        {
            btnLogin.IsEnabled = false;
            await CheckExistingProfileAndSave(entryExisting
            Email.Text);
        }
        else
        {
            await App.Current.MainPage.DisplayAlert("Error",
            "No internet connection.", "OK");
        }
    }

    btnLogin.IsEnabled = true;
}
```

The **OnbtnLoginClicked** event is also an asynchronous event that returns **void.** This event is where the user credential is validated: in this case, the e-mail address value. The first line of code within the event handler checks for the e-mail address value. If it's empty, then it displays an error; otherwise, it saves the challenger information to the local data storage by calling the **CheckExistingProfileAndSave()** method.

The Home Page

Add a new **Content Page** under the **Pages** folder and name it "**Home**". Replace the default generated code with the following code:

```
<?xml version="1.0" encoding="utf-8" ?>
<ContentPage xmlns="http://xamarin.com/schemas/2014/forms"
             xmlns:x="http://schemas.microsoft.com/winfx/2009/
             xaml"
             x:Class="MemoryGame.App.Pages.Home">

    <StackLayout Padding="2">
        <StackLayout>
            <StackLayout Orientation="Horizontal">

                <Label x:Name="lblBest"
                       FontSize="Medium"
                       HorizontalOptions="StartAndExpand" />

                <Button x:Name="btnSync"
                        Text="Sync"
                        Clicked="OnbtnSyncClicked"
                        HorizontalOptions="EndAndExpand"
                        VerticalOptions="CenterAndExpand" />

                <Button x:Name="btnLogOut"
                        Text="Logout"
                        Clicked="OnbtnLogoutClicked"
```

```
                HorizontalOptions="EndAndExpand"
                VerticalOptions="CenterAndExpand" />

    </StackLayout>

    <Label x:Name="lblTime"
           FontSize="Large"
           HorizontalOptions="Center"
           VerticalOptions="CenterAndExpand" />
</StackLayout>

<Label x:Name="lblLevel"
       FontSize="Small"
       HorizontalOptions="Center"
       VerticalOptions="CenterAndExpand" />

<StackLayout Orientation="Horizontal"
             Spacing="2"
             HorizontalOptions="Center"
             BackgroundColor="White">

    <Image x:Name="imgLightOff"
           Source="lightoff.png"
           WidthRequest="60"
           HeightRequest="20" />

    <Image x:Name="imgLightOff2"
           Source="lightoff.png"
           IsVisible="False"
           WidthRequest="60"
           HeightRequest="20" />

    <Image x:Name="imgLightOn"
           Source="lighton.png"
           IsVisible="False"
```

```
                   WidthRequest="60"
                   HeightRequest="20" />

            <Image x:Name="imgSpeaker"
                   Source="speakeron.png"
                   WidthRequest="60"
                   HeightRequest="40" />

            <Image x:Name="imgHaptic"
                   Source="vibration.png"
                   WidthRequest="60"
                   HeightRequest="20" />

        </StackLayout>

        <Label Text="The light will blink on, the speaker will
        beep and the device will vibrate at different times.
        Try to count how many times each one happens."
               HorizontalOptions="Center"
               VerticalOptions="CenterAndExpand" />

        <Button x:Name="btnStart"
                Text="Start"
                HorizontalOptions="Center"
                VerticalOptions="CenterAndExpand"
                Clicked="OnButtonClicked"/>

    </StackLayout>

</ContentPage>
```

The preceding XAML markup contains three **Label**, three **Button**, and five **Image**. The **Label** elements are used for displaying the existing saved top score, the current top score, and the instructions to play the game. The **Button** elements are used for syncing data to the database, logging out, and starting the game. The **Image** elements are used for displaying a bulb (on and off), speaker, and haptic indication.

Open the **Home.xaml.cs** file and replace the default generated code with the following code:

```
using MemoryGame.App.Classes;
using MemoryGame.App.Helper;
using MemoryGame.App.Services;
using System;
using System.Threading.Tasks;
using Xamarin.Forms;
using Xamarin.Forms.Xaml;

namespace MemoryGame.App.Pages
{
    [XamlCompilation(XamlCompilationOptions.Compile)]
    public partial class Home : ContentPage
    {
        public Home()
        {
            InitializeComponent();
        }
        enum PlayType
        {
            Blink = 0,
            Sound = 1,
            Haptic = 2
        }
        private int _cycleStartInMS = 0;
        private int _cycleMaxInMS = 10000;
        private const int _cycleIntervalInMS = 2000;
        private const int _eventTypeCount = 3;

        public statici nt CurrentGameBlinkCount { get; private
        set; } = 0;
```

```
public static int CurrentGameSoundCount { get; private
set; } = 0;
public static int CurrentGameHapticCount { get; private
set; } = 0;
public static int CurrentGameLevel { get; private set;
} = 1;

protected override void OnAppearing()
{
    base.OnAppearing();
    NavigationPage.SetHasBackButton(this, false);

    PlayerManager.UpdateBest(CurrentGameLevel);

    if (Result._answered)
        LevelUp();
    else
        ResetLevel();

    lblBest.Text = $"Best: Level {PlayerManager.GetBest
    Score(CurrentGameLevel)}";
    lblLevel.Text = $"Level {CurrentGameLevel}";
}
static void IncrementPlayCount(PlayType play)
{
   switch (play)
   {
       case PlayType.Blink:
          {
               CurrentGameBlinkCount++;
               break;
          }
       case PlayType.Sound:
          {
```

```
                CurrentGameSoundCount++;
                break;
            }
        case PlayType.Haptic:
            {
                CurrentGameHapticCount++;
                break;
            }
    }
}

public static void IncrementGameLevel()
{
    CurrentGameLevel++;
}
void ResetLevel()
{
    CurrentGameLevel = 1;
    _cycleStartInMS = _cycleIntervalInMS;
    lblTime.Text = string.Empty;
    btnStart.Text = "Start";
    btnStart.IsEnabled = true;
}
async void StartRandomPlay()
{
    await Task.Run(() =>
    {
        Random rnd = new Random(Guid.NewGuid().GetHashCode());
        int choice = rnd.Next(0, _eventTypeCount);
        switch (choice)
        {
            case (int)PlayType.Blink:
```

```
                    {
                        Device.BeginInvokeOnMainThread(async () =>
                        {
                          await imgLightOff.FadeTo(0, 200);
                          imgLightOff2.IsVisible = false;
                          imgLightOff.IsVisible = true;
                          imgLightOff.Source = ImageSource.
                          FromFile("lighton.png");
                          await imgLightOff.FadeTo(1, 200);
                        });

                        IncrementPlayCount(PlayType.Blink);
                        break;
                    }
                case (int)PlayType.Sound:
                    {
                        DependencyService.Get<ISound>().
                        PlayMp3File("beep.mp3");
                        IncrementPlayCount(PlayType.Sound);
                        break;
                    }
                case (int)PlayType.Haptic:
                    {
                        DependencyService.Get<IHaptic>().
                        ActivateHaptic();
                        IncrementPlayCount(PlayType.Haptic);
                        break;
                    }
            }
        });
    }
```

```
void ResetGameCount()
{
    CurrentGameBlinkCount = 0;
    CurrentGameSoundCount = 0;
    CurrentGameHapticCount = 0;
}

void LevelUp()
{
    _cycleStartInMS = _cycleStartInMS - 200;
    //minus 200 ms
}

void Play()
{
    int timeLapsed = 0;
    int duration = 0;
    Device.StartTimer(TimeSpan.FromSeconds(1), () =>
    {
        duration++;
        lblTime.Text = $"Timer: { TimeSpan.
        FromSeconds(duration).ToString("ss")}";

        if (duration < 10)
            return true;
        else
            return false;
    });

    Device.StartTimer(TimeSpan.FromMilliseconds(_
    cycleStartInMS), () => {
        timeLapsed = timeLapsed + _cycleStartInMS;
```

```
                Device.BeginInvokeOnMainThread(async () =>
                {
                    imgLightOff2.IsVisible = true;
                    imgLightOff.IsVisible = false;
                    await Task.Delay(200);
                });

                if (timeLapsed <= _cycleMaxInMS)
                {
                    StartRandomPlay();
                    return true; //continue
                }

                App._navPage.PushAsync(App._resultPage);
                    return false; //don't continue
            });
        }

        void OnButtonClicked(object sender, EventArgs args)
        {
            btnStart.Text = "Game Started...";
            btnStart.IsEnabled = false;

            ResetGameCount();

            Play();
        }

       async void OnbtnSyncClicked(object sender, EventArgs args)
        {
            if (Utils.IsConnectedToInternet())
            {
                btnSync.Text = "Syncing...";
                btnSync.IsEnabled = false;
                btnStart.IsEnabled = false;

                var response = await PlayerManager.Sync();
```

```
            if (!response)
                await App.Current.MainPage.
                DisplayAlert("Oops", "An error occurred
                while connecting to the server. Please
                check your connection.", "OK");
            else
                await App.Current.MainPage.
                DisplayAlert("Sync", "Data synced!","OK");
            btnSync.Text = "Sync";
            btnSync.IsEnabled = true;
            btnStart.IsEnabled = true;
        }
        else
        {
            await App.Current.MainPage.DisplayAlert
            ("Error", "No internet connection.", "OK");
        }
    }
    async void OnbtnLogoutClicked(object sender, EventArgs
    args)
    {
        if (Utils.IsConnectedToInternet())
        {
            btnLogOut.IsEnabled = false;
            var response = await PlayerManager.Sync();

            if (response)
            {
                Settings.ClearEverything();
                await App._navPage.PopToRootAsync();
            }
```

```
                else
                    await App.Current.MainPage.
                    DisplayAlert("Oops","An error occurred
                    while connecting to the server. Please
                    check your connection.", "OK");
            }
            else

                    await App.Current.MainPage.DisplayAlert
                    ("Oops", "No internet connection. Please
                    check your network.", "OK");

            btnLogOut.IsEnabled = true;

        }

    }
}
```

The code-behind for the **Home** page is expected to be long, because this is where the game logic is handled. I keep it this way in order for you to easily reference the relevant code logic in one place and for simplicity's sake. In a real-world scenario, you may want to break the code into classes and identify components that can be reusable.

Let's see what the code does by breaking it into sections. Let's start with the class-level definition:

```
[XamlCompilation(XamlCompilationOptions.Compile)]
public partial class Home : ContentPage
{
    public Home()
    {
        InitializeComponent();
    }
}
```

Just like any other XAML page, the **Home** class inherits the ContentPage class. Within the class constructor, it calls the method **InitializeComponent()** to initialize a new **ContentPage** instance.

Next code block:

```
enum PlayType
{
    Blink = 0,
    Sound = 1,
    Haptic = 2
}
```

The **PlayType** is an **enum** that consists of three main entries: Blink, Sound, and Haptic. This enum will be used later in the code to identify the type of event played.

Next code block:

```
private int _cycleStartInMS = 0;
private int _cycleMaxInMS = 10000;
private const int _cycleIntervalInMS = 2000;
private const int _eventTypeCount = 3;
```

The preceding code comprises the **private** global variables of type **int** that will be used within the class. The _cycleStartInMS variable value is expressed in milliseconds and defaults to 0. This variable indicates the time when the app should trigger a new cycle to start the play. The cycleMaxInMS variable indicates the maximum time to when the app stops the play. The default value is 10,000 milliseconds, or 10 seconds. The last two variables are marked as **const**, meaning the value assigned to them won't change. The _cycleIntervalInMS variable indicates the time interval between playing different event types such as blinking an image, playing a sound, or activating vibration on the device. The interval value is 2000 milliseconds, equivalent to 2 seconds. The eventTypeCount variable indicates the number of event types, for which the value in this case is 3.

Next code block:

```
public static int CurrentGameBlinkCount { get; privateset; } = 0;
public static int CurrentGameSoundCount { get; privateset; } = 0;
public static int CurrentGameHapticCount { get; privateset; } = 0;
public static int CurrentGameLevel { get; privateset; } = 1;
```

The preceding code comprises the public properties for the class. They are marked **public** and **static,** so other class can access them without having to create an instance of the **Home** class. The preceding syntax uses property initializers, which was introduced in C# 6.0.

The CurrentGameBlinkCount property holds the number of **blink** counts with the default value of 0. The CurrentGameSoundCount property holds the number of **sound** counts with the default value of 0. The CurrentGameHapticCount property holds the number of **haptic** counts with the default value of 0. Last but not least, the CurrentGameLevel holds the level/score value.

Next code block:

```
protected override void OnAppearing()
{
    base.OnAppearing();
    NavigationPage.SetHasBackButton(this, false);

    PlayerManager.UpdateBest(CurrentGameLevel);

    if (Result._answered)
        LevelUp();
    else
        ResetLevel();

    lblBest.Text = $"Best: Level {PlayerManager.GetBestScore
    (CurrentGameLevel)}";
    lblLevel.Text = $"Level {CurrentGameLevel}";
}
```

The **OnAppearing()** method fires before the page gets visible. The preceding code disables the back navigation of the app and then updates the challenger top score. The if-condition checks the value of _answered from the Result page. If true, then it calls the **LevelUp()** method, otherwise it calls the **ResetLevel()**.

The last two lines of code within the method sets the label's **Text** property to display the top score and current score.

Next code block:

```
static void IncrementPlayCount(PlayType play)
{
    switch (play)
    {
        case PlayType.Blink:
        {
            CurrentGameBlinkCount++;
            break;
        }
        case PlayType.Sound:
            {
                CurrentGameSoundCount++;
                break;
            }
        case PlayType.Haptic:
            {
                CurrentGameHapticCount++;
                break;
            }
    }
}
```

The IncrementPlayCount() method takes a **PlayType** object as a parameter. This method basically increases the number of each event type based on the enum value.

Next code block:

```
public static void IncrementGameLevel()
{
    CurrentGameLevel++;
}
```

The IncrementGameLevel() increases the level/score value. This method is marked as public so other class can invoke it.

Next code block:

```
void ResetLevel()
{
    CurrentGameLevel = 1;
    _cycleStartInMS = _cycleIntervalInMS;
    lblTime.Text = string.Empty;
}
```

The ResetLevel() method resets the level/score and play cycle time and clears the time displayed in the view.

Next code block:

```
async void StartRandomPlay()
{
    await Task.Run(() =>
    {
        Random rnd = new Random(Guid.NewGuid().GetHashCode());
        int choice = rnd.Next(0, _eventTypeCount);

        switch (choice)
        {
            case (int)PlayType.Blink:
```

```
                {
                    Device.BeginInvokeOnMainThread(async () =>
                    {
                            await imgLightOff.FadeTo(0, 200);
                            imgLightOff2.IsVisible = false;
                            imgLightOff.IsVisible = true;
                            imgLightOff.Source = ImageSource.
                            FromFile("lighton.png");
                            await imgLightOff.FadeTo(1, 200);
                    });

                    IncrementPlayCount(PlayType.Blink);
                    break;
                }
            case (int)PlayType.Sound:
                {
                    DependencyService.Get<ISound>().
                    PlayMp3File("beep.mp3");
                    IncrementPlayCount(PlayType.Sound);
                    break;
                }
            case (int)PlayType.Haptic:
                {
                    DependencyService.Get<IHaptic>().
                    ActivateHaptic();
                    IncrementPlayCount(PlayType.Haptic);
                    break;
                }
        }
    });
}
```

The StartRandomPlay() is an asynchronous method that returns a **void**. The preceding code is the core method of the **Home** class. The method is responsible for activating different criteria on a random basis, whether invoking a sound, making a vibration, or just blinking an image. Notice that we've used the **DependencyService** class to inject the interface that we've defined in previous section of this Chapter. This allows us to perform platform specific implementations for playing a sound or activating a device vibration.

Next code block:

```
void ResetGameCount()
{
    CurrentGameBlinkCount = 0;
    CurrentGameSoundCount = 0;
    CurrentGameHapticCount = 0;
}
```

The preceding code simply resets the properties value to 0.

Next code block:

```
void LevelUp()
{
    _cycleStartInMS = _cycleStartInMS - 200; //minus 200 ms
}
```

The preceding code decreases the cycle interval for triggering a new random event. In other words, the 2-second cycle will be decreased by 200 ms per level. This is where the game gets exciting, because the higher your level/score goes, the faster the different event types are triggered until you can't remember which type of event has occurred.

Next code block:

```
void Play()
{
    int timeLapsed = 0;
    int duration = 0;
    Device.StartTimer(TimeSpan.FromSeconds(1), () =>
    {
        duration++;
        lblTime.Text = $"Timer: { TimeSpan.
        FromSeconds(duration).ToString("ss")}";

        if (duration < 10)
            return true;
        else
            return false;
        });

        Device.StartTimer(TimeSpan.FromMilliseconds
        (_cycleStartInMS), () => {
            timeLapsed = timeLapsed + _cycleStartInMS;

            Device.BeginInvokeOnMainThread(async () =>
            {
                imgLightOff2.IsVisible = true;
                imgLightOff.IsVisible = false;
                await Task.Delay(200);
            });
            if (timeLapsed <= _cycleMaxInMS)
            {
                StartRandomPlay();
                return true; //continue
            }
```

```
            App._navPage.PushAsync(App._resultPage);
            return false; //don't continue
        });
}
```

The preceding code invokes two methods for starting a timer on the view. The **Device.StartTimer()** starts a recurring timer on the UI thread using the device clock capabilities. The first one creates a countdown timer in the view starting from 10 seconds to 0 and displays the result to a **Label** element in real time. The second invokation of the **Device.StartTimer()** method is responsible for triggering a new random event based in the current value of the _cycleMaxInMS value.

Next code block:

```
void OnButtonClicked(object sender, EventArgs args)
{
    btnStart.Text = "Game Started...";
    btnStart.IsEnabled = false;

    ResetGameCount();

    Play();
}
```

The **OnButtonClicked** event activates and starts the game by calling the **Play()** method.

Next code block:

```
async void OnbtnSyncClicked(object sender, EventArgs args)
{
    if (Utils.IsConnectedToInternet())
    {
        btnSync.Text = "Syncing...";
        btnSync.IsEnabled = false;
        btnStart.IsEnabled = false;
```

```
        var response = await PlayerManager.Sync();
        if (!response)
            await App.Current.MainPage
                  DisplayAlert("Oops"
                  "An error occurred while connecting to the
                  server. Please check your connection.", "OK");
        else
            await App.Current.MainPage.DisplayAlert("Sync",
            "Data synced!","OK");

        btnSync.Text = "Sync";
        btnSync.IsEnabled = true;
        btnStart.IsEnabled = true;
    }
    else
    {
        await App.Current.MainPage
                  DisplayAlert("Error"
                  "No internet connection."
                  "OK");
    }
}
```

The **OnbtnSyncClicked()** is an asynchronous event handler that syncs data to the database. The first line of the code within the method checks for the connection using the Utils.IsConnectedToInternet() method. If the device is connected to an Internet or wifi, then it enables data sync by calling the awaitable **Sync()** method from the **PlayerManager** class.

Next code block:

```
async void OnbtnLogoutClicked(object sender, EventArgs args)
{
    if (Utils.IsConnectedToInternet())
    {
```

```
        btnLogOut.IsEnabled = false;
        var response = await PlayerManager.Sync();
        if (response)
        {
            Settings.ClearEverything();
            await App._navPage.PopToRootAsync();
        }
        else
            await App.Current.MainPage
                  DisplayAlert("Oops"
                  "An error occurred while connecting to the
                  server. Please check your connection."
                  "OK");
    }
    else
        await App.Current.MainPage
                  DisplayAlert("Oops"
                  "No internet connection. Please check your
                  network."
                  "OK");

    btnLogOut.IsEnabled = true;
}
```

The OnbtnLogoutClicked event handles the logout functionality of the application. Just like the sync feature, it first checks for Internet connectivity. If the device is connected, it will then invoke the **Sync()** method to persist the data in the database. If it syncs successfully, then it clears the data from the local device storage using the Settings. ClearEverything() method and redirects the user back to the default page.

The Result Page

Add a new **Content Page** under the **Pages** folder and name it "**Result**". Replace the default generated code with the following code:

```
<?xml version="1.0" encoding="utf-8" ?>
<ContentPage xmlns="http://xamarin.com/schemas/2014/forms"
             xmlns:x="http://schemas.microsoft.com/winfx/2009/
             xaml"
             x:Class="MemoryGame.App.Pages.Result">

    <StackLayout>

        <Label Text="How many times did the light blink, the
        speaker beep and the device vibrate?"
               HorizontalOptions="Center"
               VerticalOptions="CenterAndExpand" />

        <StackLayout Orientation="Horizontal"
             Spacing="2"
             HorizontalOptions="Center"
             BackgroundColor="White">

            <Image x:Name="imgLight"
                   Source="lightoff.png"
                   WidthRequest="60"
                   HeightRequest="20" />

            <Image x:Name="imgSpeaker"
                   Source="speakeron.png"
                   WidthRequest="60"
                   HeightRequest="20" />

            <Image x:Name="imgHaptic"
```

```
                Source="vibration.png"
                WidthRequest="60"
                HeightRequest="20" />

        </StackLayout>

        <StackLayout Orientation="Horizontal"
                     HorizontalOptions="Center"
                     Spacing="5">

            <Picker x:Name="pickerLight"
                    HorizontalOptions="FillAndExpand"
                    WidthRequest="100">
                <Picker.Items>
                    <x:String>0</x:String>
                    <x:String>1</x:String>
                    <x:String>2</x:String>
                    <x:String>3</x:String>
                    <x:String>4</x:String>
                    <x:String>5</x:String>
                    <x:String>6</x:String>
                    <x:String>7</x:String>
                    <x:String>8</x:String>
                    <x:String>9</x:String>
                    <x:String>10</x:String>
                </Picker.Items>
            </Picker>

            <Picker x:Name="pickerSpeaker"
                    HorizontalOptions="FillAndExpand"
                    WidthRequest="100">
                <Picker.Items>
                    <x:String>0</x:String>
```

```
            <x:String>1</x:String>
            <x:String>2</x:String>
            <x:String>3</x:String>
            <x:String>4</x:String>
            <x:String>5</x:String>
            <x:String>6</x:String>
            <x:String>7</x:String>
            <x:String>8</x:String>
            <x:String>9</x:String>
            <x:String>10</x:String>
        </Picker.Items>
    </Picker>

    <Picker x:Name="pickerHaptic"
            HorizontalOptions="FillAndExpand"
            WidthRequest="100">
        <Picker.Items>
            <x:String>0</x:String>
            <x:String>1</x:String>
            <x:String>2</x:String>
            <x:String>3</x:String>
            <x:String>4</x:String>
            <x:String>5</x:String>
            <x:String>6</x:String>
            <x:String>7</x:String>
            <x:String>8</x:String>
            <x:String>9</x:String>
            <x:String>10</x:String>
        </Picker.Items>
    </Picker>

</StackLayout>
```

```
<Label x:Name="lblText"
        FontSize="20"
        HorizontalOptions="Center"
        VerticalOptions="CenterAndExpand" />

<StackLayout Orientation="Horizontal"
             HorizontalOptions="Center"
             Spacing="40">

    <Label x:Name="lblBlinkCount"
           HorizontalOptions="Center"
           VerticalOptions="CenterAndExpand" />

    <Label x:Name="lblBeepCount"
           HorizontalOptions="Center"
           VerticalOptions="CenterAndExpand" />

    <Label x:Name="lblHapticCount"
           HorizontalOptions="Center"
           VerticalOptions="CenterAndExpand" />

</StackLayout>

<Button x:Name="btnSubmit"
        Text="Submit"
        HorizontalOptions="Center"
        VerticalOptions="CenterAndExpand"
        Clicked="OnButtonClicked"/>

<Button x:Name="btnRetry"
        Text="Retry"
        IsVisible="False"
        HorizontalOptions="Center"
        VerticalOptions="CenterAndExpand"
```

```
                Clicked="OnRetryButtonClicked"/>

    </StackLayout>

</ContentPage>
```

The preceding XAML markup contains a few **Label, Button, Picker** and **Image** elements. The **Picker** elements are used for storing a list of items for a challenger to pick. The **Label** elements are used for displaying the answer count for each event type that has occurred. The **Button** elements are used for submitting the answers or navigating back to the **Home** page to restart the game. The **Image** elements are used for displaying a bulb, a speaker, and a haptic indication.

Open the **Result.xaml.cs** file and replace the default generated code with the following code:

```
using MemoryGame.App.Classes;
using System;
using Xamarin.Forms;
using Xamarin.Forms.Xaml;

namespace MemoryGame.App.Pages
{
    [XamlCompilation(XamlCompilationOptions.Compile)]
        public partial class Result : ContentPage
        {
          public static bool _answered = false;
          public Result()
          {
              InitializeComponent();
              ClearResult();
          }

          protected override void OnAppearing()
          {
```

```
    base.OnAppearing();
    ClearResult();
    NavigationPage.SetHasBackButton(this, false);
}
void ClearResult()
{
    lblText.Text = string.Empty;
    lblBlinkCount.Text = string.Empty;
    lblBeepCount.Text = string.Empty;
    lblHapticCount.Text = string.Empty;
    pickerLight.SelectedIndex = 0;
    pickerSpeaker.SelectedIndex = 0;
    pickerHaptic.SelectedIndex = 0;
    btnSubmit.IsVisible = true;
    btnRetry.IsVisible = false;
    _answered = false;
}

bool CheckAnswer(int actualAnswer, int selectedAnswer)
{
    if (selectedAnswer == actualAnswer)
        return true;
    else
        return false;
}

void Retry()
{
    btnSubmit.IsVisible = false;
    btnRetry.IsVisible = true;
}

async void OnButtonClicked(object sender, EventArgs args)
```

```
{
    if (pickerLight.SelectedIndex >= 0 &&
    pickerSpeaker.SelectedIndex >= 0 && pickerHaptic.
    SelectedIndex >= 0)
    {
        lblText.Text = "The actual answers are:";
        lblBlinkCount.Text = Home.
        CurrentGameBlinkCount.ToString();
        lblBeepCount.Text = Home.
        CurrentGameSoundCount.ToString();
        lblHapticCount.Text = Home.
        CurrentGameHapticCount.ToString();

        int blinkCountAnswer = Convert.ToInt32
        (pickerLight.Items[pickerLight.SelectedIndex]);
        int soundCountAnswer = Convert.ToInt32
        (pickerSpeaker.Items[pickerSpeaker.SelectedIndex]);
        int hapticCountAnswer = Convert.ToInt32
        (pickerHaptic.Items[pickerHaptic.SelectedIndex]);

        if (CheckAnswer(Home.CurrentGameBlinkCount,
        blinkCountAnswer))
            if (CheckAnswer(Home.CurrentGameSoundCount,
            soundCountAnswer))
                if (CheckAnswer(Home.CurrentGame
                HapticCount,hapticCountAnswer))
                {
                    _answered = true;
                    Home.IncrementGameLevel();

                    var isSynced = PlayerManager.Check
                    ScoreAndSync(Home.CurrentGameLevel);
```

```
                    var answer = await App.Current.
                    MainPage.DisplayAlert("Congrats!",
                    $"You've got it all right and made
                    it to level {Home.CurrentGameLevel}.
                    Continue?", "Yes", "No");

                    if (answer)
                    await App._navPage.PopAsync();
                else
                    Retry();
            }
        if (!_answered)
        {
            var isSynced = PlayerManager.
            CheckScoreAndSync(Home.CurrentGameLevel);

            var answer = await App.Current.MainPage.
            DisplayAlert("Game Over!", $"Your current
            best is at level{Home.CurrentGameLevel}.
            Retry?", "Yes", "No");
            if (answer)
                await App._navPage.PopAsync();
            else
                Retry();
        }
    }
}
void OnRetryButtonClicked(object sender, EventArgs args)
{
    App._navPage.PopAsync();
}
}
}
```

The preceding code handles the logic for validating the answers against the actual count of each event type occurred. If all answers are correct, then it will prompt you with a message asking if you want to proceed to the next level or not.

Setting the Page Navigation

Now that we have the required pages set up, let's declare them on the **App** class to create a simple navigation with a default page.

Go ahead and open the **App.xaml.cs** file and replace the existing code with the following code:

```
using MemoryGame.App.Pages;
using Xamarin.Forms;
using Xamarin.Forms.Xaml;

[assembly: XamlCompilation(XamlCompilationOptions.Compile)]
namespace MemoryGame.App
{
    public partial class App : Application
    {
        public static NavigationPage _navPage;
        public static Home _homePage;
        public static Result _resultPage;
        public static Register _registerPage;

        public App()
        {
            InitializeComponent();
            _homePage = new Home();
            _resultPage = new Result();
            _registerPage = new Register();
            _navPage = new NavigationPage(_registerPage);
```

```
            MainPage = _navPage;
        }

        protected override void OnStart()
        {
            // Handle when your app starts
        }

        protected override void OnSleep()
        {
            // Handle when your app sleeps
        }

        protected override void OnResume()
        {
            // Handle when your app resumes
        }
    }
}
```

The **App** class inherits the **Application** base class, which offers the following features:

- A **MainPage** property, which is where to set the initial page for the app.
- A persistent **Properties** dictionary to store simple values across lifecycle state changes.
- A static **Current** property that contains a reference to the current application object.

The code within the app class defines a public static **NavigationPage** object and the three **Pages** that we've created in the previous section: **Register**, **Home**, and **Result**. These objects are then **initialized** in the class contractor with the default page set to the **Register** page. The **MainPage** property on the application class sets the root page of the application.

***For more information about the Xamarin.Forms app class, see the following:* `https://docs.microsoft.com/en-us/xamarin/xamarin-forms/app-fundamentals/application-class`**

Summary of Files Added

Here's what the MemoryGame.App project looks like after all the files are added.

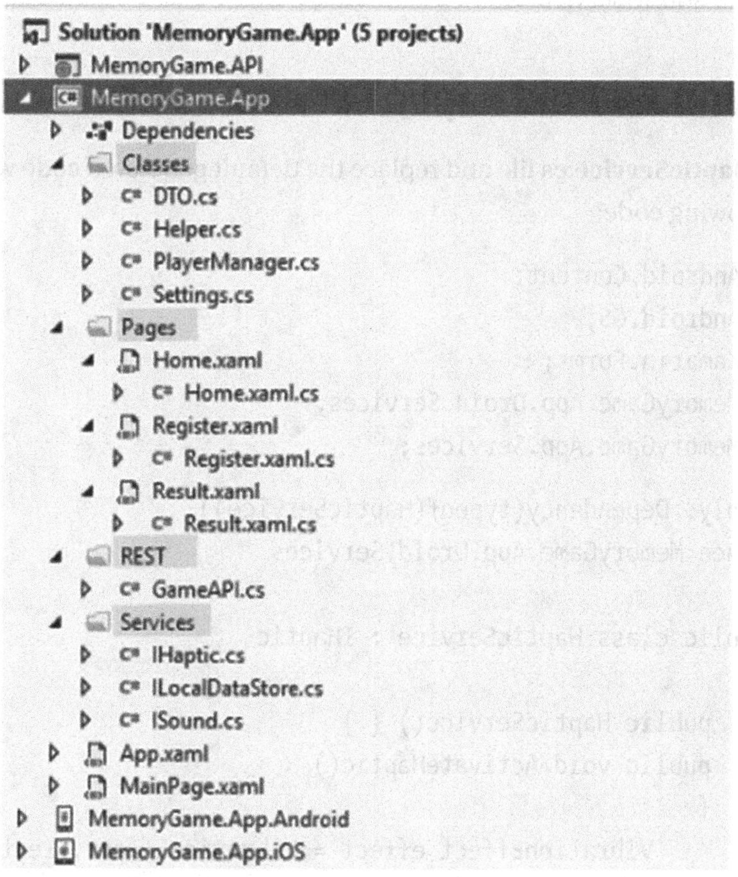

Figure 4-6. *Summary of newly added files*

Implementing the Haptic and Sound Services

Now it's time for us to provide an actual implementation of each interface created in previous sections of this chapter. Let's start with the Xamain. Android. Add a new folder called "**Services**" in the **MemoryGame.App. Android** project and then create the following classes:

- HapticServer.cs
- SoundService.cs

Xamarin.Android Haptic Service

Open **HapticService.cs** file and replace the default generated code with the following code:

```
using Android.Content;
using Android.OS;
using Xamarin.Forms;
using MemoryGame.App.Droid.Services;
using MemoryGame.App.Services;

[assembly: Dependency(typeof(HapticService))]
namespace MemoryGame.App.Droid.Services
{
    public class HapticService : IHaptic
    {
        public HapticService() { }
        public void ActivateHaptic()
        {
            VibrationEffect effect = VibrationEffect.CreateOne
            Shot(100, VibrationEffect.DefaultAmplitude);
```

```
                Vibrator vibrator = (Vibrator)global::Android.App.
                Application.Context.GetSystemService
                (Context.VibratorService);
                vibrator.Vibrate(effect);
            }
        }
    }
```

The **HapticService** class implements the **ActivateHaptic()** method of the **IHaptic** interface. The preceding code contains Android-specific implementation for activating the device vibration.

Xamarin.Android Sound Service

Open **SoundService.cs** file and replace the default generated code with the following code:

```
using Xamarin.Forms;
using Android.Media;
using MemoryGame.App.Droid.Services;
using MemoryGame.App.Services;

[assembly: Dependency(typeof(SoundService))]

namespace MemoryGame.App.Droid.Services
{
    public class SoundService : ISound
    {
        public SoundService() { }

        private MediaPlayer _mediaPlayer;

        public bool PlayMp3File(string fileName)
        {
            _mediaPlayer = MediaPlayer.Create(Android.App.
            Application.Context, Resource.Raw.beep);
```

```
            _mediaPlayer.Start();

            return true;
        }

        public bool PlayWavFile(string fileName)
        {
            //TO DO: Own implementation here
            return true;
        }
    }
}
```

The **SoundService** class implements the **PlayMp3File()** method of the **ISound** interface. The preceding code contains Android-specific implementation for playing a media.

Now switch to the **MemoryGame.App.iOS** project. Add a new folder called "**Services**" and then create the following classes:

- HapticServer.cs
- SoundService.cs

Xamarin.iOS Haptic Service

Open the **HapticService.cs** file and replace the default generated code with the following code:

```
using Xamarin.Forms;
using AudioToolbox;
using MemoryGame.App.iOS.Services;
using MemoryGame.App.Services;
```

```
[assembly: Dependency(typeof(HapticService))]
namespace MemoryGame.App.iOS.Services
{
    public class HapticService : IHaptic
    {
        public HapticService() { }
        public void ActivateHaptic()
        {
            SystemSound.Vibrate.PlaySystemSound();
        }
    }
}
```

The preceding code contains iOS-specific implementation for activating device vibration. It uses the **SystemSound.Vibrate.PlaySystemSound()** to vibrate the device in iOS.

Xamarin.iOS Sound Service

Open the **SoundService.cs** file and replace the default generated code with the following code:

```
using Xamarin.Forms;
using MemoryGame.App.iOS.Services;
using System.IO;
using Foundation;
using AVFoundation;
using MemoryGame.App.Services;
```

```
[assembly: Dependency(typeof(SoundService))]
namespace MemoryGame.App.iOS.Services
{
    public class SoundService : NSObject, ISound,
    IAVAudioPlayerDelegate
    {
        public SoundService(){}
        public bool PlayWavFile(string fileName)
        {
            return true;
        }
        public bool PlayMp3File(string fileName)
        {
            var played = false;
            NSError error = null;
            AVAudioSession.SharedInstance().SetCategory
            (AVAudioSession.CategoryPlayback, out error);
            string sFilePath = NSBundle.MainBundle.
            PathForResource
            (Path.GetFileNameWithoutExtension(fileName),
            "mp3");
            var url = NSUrl.FromString(sFilePath);
            var _player = AVAudioPlayer.FromUrl(url);
            _player.Delegate = this;
            _player.Volume = 100f;
            played = _player.PrepareToPlay();
            _player.FinishedPlaying += (object sender,
            AVStatusEventArgs e) => {
            _player = null;
            };
```

```
            played = _player.Play();
            return played;
        }
    }
}
```

The **SoundService** class implements the **PlayMp3File()** method of the **ISound** interface. The preceding code contains iOS-specific implementation for playing a media.

Note For iOS, add the required images and sound file under the Resource folder.

Setting Permissions

Xamarin.Android

For Android, open the AndroidManifest.xml file as shown in the following figure:

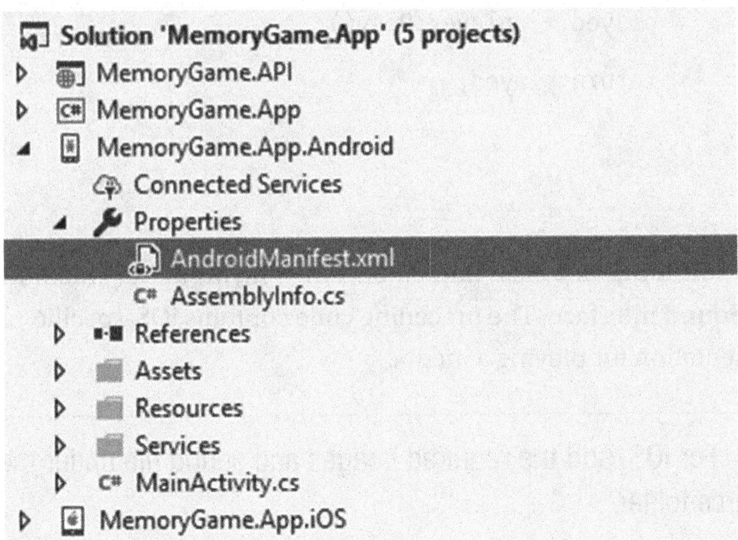

Figure 4-7. The AndroidManifest.xml file

Then, add the following configuration:

```
<uses-permission android:name="android.permission.VIBRATE" />
<uses-permission android:name="android.permission.ACCESS_
                                 NETWORK_STATE" />
<uses-permission android:name="android.permission.ACCESS_WIFI_
                                 STATE" />
<uses-permission android:name="android.permission.INTERNET" />
```

Xamarin.iOS

An iOS device doesn't require any permissions. In Android, the system seeks the user's permission while the app is being installed. But iOS allows you to go ahead with an installation, seeking permission when the user is using a feature that requires specific permission.

Note Apple has made several enhancements to both security and privacy in iOS 10 (and greater) that will help the developer improve the security of their apps and ensure the end user's privacy. For the new iOS 10 Privacy Permission Settings, see: `https://blog.xamarin.com/new-ios-10-privacy-permission-settings/`

CHAPTER 5

Building a Simple Real-Time Leaderboard Web App with ASP.NET SignalR and MVC

Before we start implementing real-time functionality, let's get to know what ASP.NET SignalR and MVC are all about. Although we are not going to fully utilize the features that the MVC framework offers, it is still nice to have a basic understanding of how the MVC framework works.

What ASP.NET MVC Is

ASP.NET MVC is part of the ASP.NET framework. The following figure will give you a high-level look at where ASP.NET MVC resides within the ASP.NET framework.

V. M. S. Durano, *Understanding Game Application Development*,
https://doi.org/10.1007/978-1-4842-4264-3_5

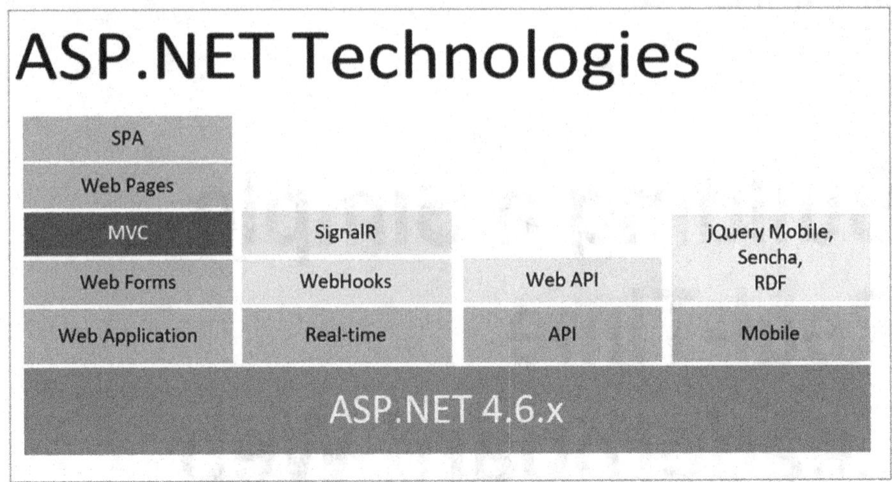

***Figure 5-1.** The ASP.NET technologies*

In the preceding figure, you see that ASP.NET MVC sits on top of ASP.NET. ASP.NET MVC is a UI framework that enables a clean separation of concerns and gives you full control over your markup.

To make it clearer, here's how I view the high-level process of MVC:

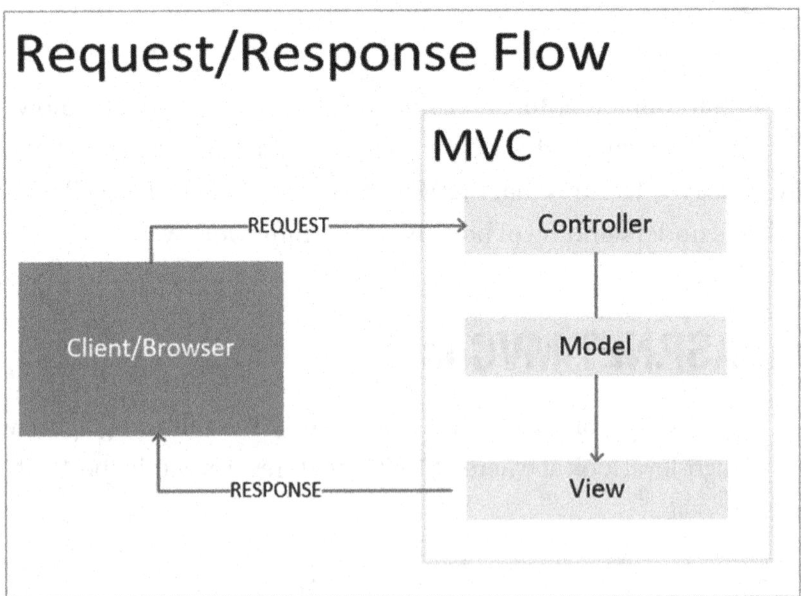

***Figure 5-2.** Request and response flow*

Unlike in ASP.NET WebForms, in which requests go directly to a page file (.ASPX), in MVC, when a user requests a page, it will first talk to the **Controller**, process data when necessary, and return a **Model** to the **View** for the user to see.

The Model

Model is just a class that implements the logic for the application domain data. Often, model objects retrieve and store model states in the database.

The Controller

Just like models, **Controller** is also a class that handles the user interaction. It will work with the model and ultimately select a view to render in the browser.

The View

As the name suggests, a **View** is the component that displays the application's UI; typically, this UI is created from the model data.

To put them up together, the **M** is for Model, which is typically where the business objects, business layer, and data access layer will live. Note that in typical layered architecture, your business layer and data access layer should be in separate projects. The **V** is for View, which is what the user sees. This could simply mean that any UI- and client-side-related developments will live in the View, including HTML, CSS, and JavaScript. The **C** is for the Controller, which orchestrates the flow of logic. For example, if a user clicks a button that points to a specific URL, that request is mapped to the controller action method that is responsible for handling any logic required to service the request and return a response. This will typically be a new view, or an update to the existing view.

***To get started with ASP.NET MVC 5, I'd recommend you read my series of article here:* `http://vmsdurano.com/building-web-application-using-entity-framework-and-mvc-5-part-1/`**

What ASP.NET SignalR Is

ASP.NET SignalR is a new library for ASP.NET developers that makes developing real-time web functionality easy. SignalR allows bidirectional communication between server and client. Servers can now push content to connected clients instantly as it becomes available. SignalR supports WebSockets and falls back to other compatible techniques for older browsers.

SignalR can be used wherever a user is required to refresh a page in order to see up-to-date data. It allows the server to logically "push" data to the client. This is typically required for web-based dashboards and monitoring tools, where information needs to be kept up to date at all times without the user having to refresh the page. SignalR is a powerful, high-level library that abstracts a lot of the complicated underlying technologies in order to provide an easy way to transmit data between the client and the server. SignalR manages the connections automatically and allows data to be sent using either broadcasts or unicasts.

In SignalR, there are two distinct models for implementing client-server communications:

- **Persistent Connections** are the base class with an API for exposing a SignalR service over HTTP. They are useful for when developers need direct access to the low-level communication technology. Persistent connections use a model similar to that of WCF.

- **Hubs** are built on top of persistent connections and abstract most of the underlying complexity in order to allow developers to call methods on both the client and the server without worrying about the implementation details. One great benefit of using Hubs is that you get model binding and serialization straight out of the box.

Transport Protocols Selection

One of the great features about SignalR is that when a client doesn't support WebSockets, it automatically falls back to using older methods of communication, as shown in the following figure:

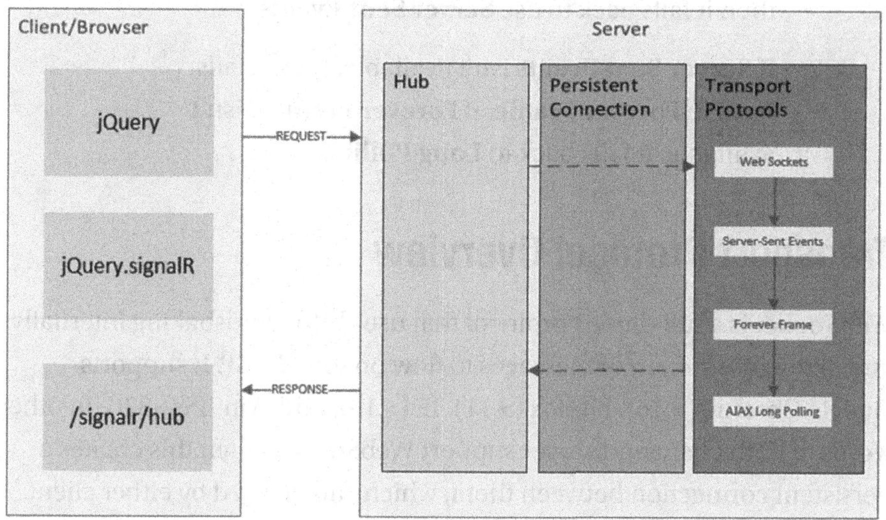

Figure 5-3. *SignalR communication flow*

SignalR is quite flexible in terms of supporting a variety of transport protocols. It uses the WebSocket transport when available, but falls back to older transports when necessary. WebSocket requires at least Windows Server 2012 or Windows 8, and .NET Framework 4.5 for server and at least IE 10 for the client. If these requirements are not met, SignalR will attempt to use other transports to make its connections.

The following are the available transport protocols:

- WebSockets
- Long Polling
- Server Sent Events
- Forever Frame

The default transport selection process goes like this:

1. If the client/server doesn't support **WebSockets**, then it falls back to use **Server Sent Events**.
2. If **Server Sent Events** isn't available, then it falls back to **Forever Frame**; if **Forever Frame** if isn't available, it falls back to **Long Polling**.

Transport Protocol Overview

WebSocket is a full duplex protocol that uses http handshaking internally and allows the stream of messages to flow on top of TCP. It supports Google Chrome (> 16), Firefox (> 11), IE (> 10), and Win IIS (>8.0). In other words, if both client and server support WebSockets, then this creates a persistent connection between them, which can be used by either client or server to send the data anytime. As such, this way is the most efficient, takes the least memory, and shows the lowest latency. This is the most preferred protocol for a SignalR application.

- **Simplex Communication**: It just spreads in one way when one point just broadcasts while another point just can listen without sending a message, such as television and radio.
- **Half Duplex**: One point sends a message and at that moment another point cannot send a message and must wait until the first point finishes its transmission; then it can send its message. It is just one communication at a time, such as old wireless devices like walkie-talkies and HTTP protocol.
- **Full Duplex**: Both points can send and receive messages simultaneously; there is no need to wait until the other point finishes its transmission. This is similar to telephones and WebSocket protocol.

Server Sent Events (also known as Event Source): This is another technique introduced with HTML5 that allows the server to push the updates to the client whenever new data is available. This technology is used when WebSocket is not supported. It is supported by most browsers except IE.

Forever Frame: This is part of the Comet model and uses a hidden iframe in the browser to receive the data in an incremental manner from the server. The server starts sending the data in a series of chunks even without even knowing the complete length of the content. It is executed on the client when the data is received.

AJAX Long Polling: This is the least preferred way in SignalR to set up a communication between client and server. Also, it is the most expensive! It is a part of the Comet model and as the name suggests, it keeps polling the server to check for updates. The request that is sent to the server is AJAX based, to minimize the resource usage and provide a better user experience. But it's still expensive because it keeps polling the server whether there are any updates or not.

For more information, see **`www.asp.net/signalr`**

Create a New Web Application

Now that you have an idea of how SignalR transmits and persists data across client and the server, it's time for us to see that in action.

Let's add a new ASP.NET web application project. Right-click the Solution and then select **Add ➤ New Project**. On the left pane under **Visual C# ➤ Web**, select **ASP.NET Web Application (.NET Framework)** and name it "**MemoryGame.Web**" just like in the following figure:

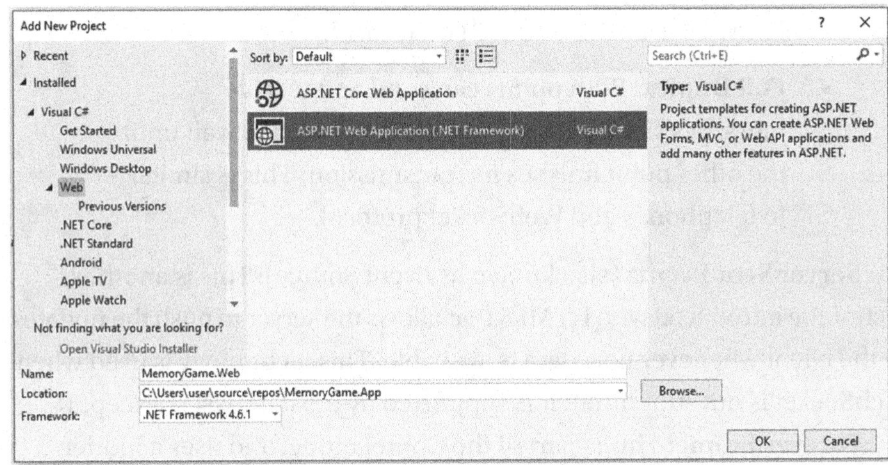

***Figure 5-4.** Create a new ASP.NET web application project*

Click **OK** and then select **Empty.** Tick the MVC option under the "Add folders and core references for:" just like in the following figure:

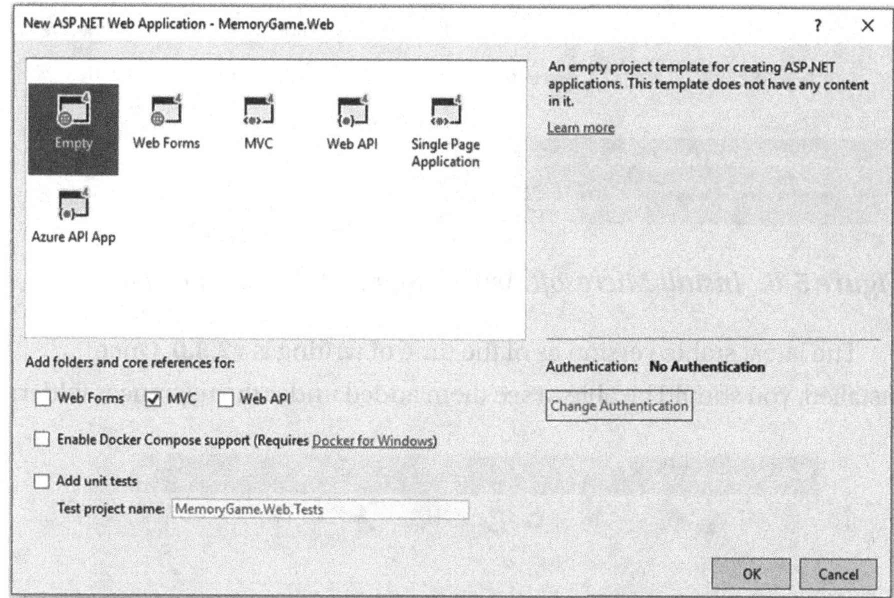

Figure 5-5. *Create an empty ASP.NET MVC project*

Click **OK** to let Visual Studio generate the project for you.

Integrating ASP.NET SignalR

Install **Microsoft.Asp.Net.SignalR** in your project via NuGet as shown the following figure:

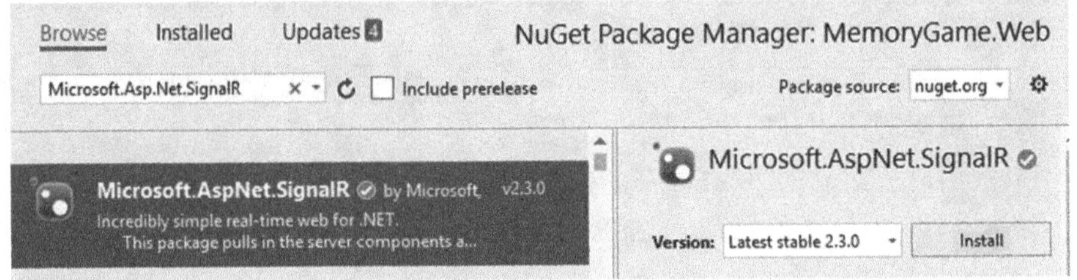

Figure 5-6. *Install Microsoft.AspNet.SignalR NuGet package*

The latest stable version as of the time of writing is **v2.3.0**. Once installed, you should be able to see them added under the references folder:

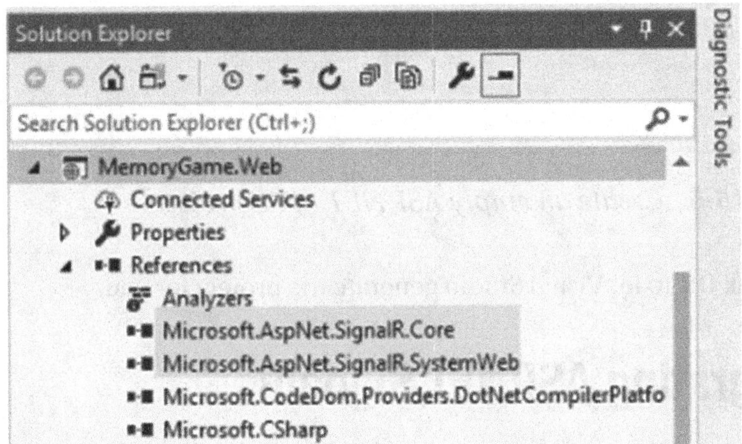

Figure 5-7. *ASP.NET SignalR references*

The **Microsoft.AspNet.SignalR.Core** is responsible for pulling in the server components and **JavaScript** client required to use **SignalR** in our application. **Microsoft.AspNet.SignalR.SystemWeb** contains components for using **SignalR** in applications hosted on **System.Web**.

Install **Microsoft.AspNet.Web.Optimization** and then add the following code under **View ➤ web.config**:

```
<addnamespace="System.Web.Optimization"/>
```

Adding a Middleware for SignalR

We need to create a middleware for SignalR so we can configure it for use by creating an **IApplicationBuilder** extension method. Create a new class at the root of the **MemoryGame.Web** project, name it "**Startup.cs**", and then replace the generated code with the following:

```
using Microsoft.Owin;
using Owin;

[assembly: OwinStartup(typeof(MemoryGame.Web.Startup))]
namespace MemoryGame.Web
{
    public class Startup
    {
        public void Configuration(IAppBuilder app)
        {
            app.MapSignalR();
        }
    }
}
```

The preceding configuration will add the **SignalR** services to the pipeline and enable us to use ASP.NET SignalR real-time capabilities in our application.

Adding a Hub

Next is to add an ASP.NET SignalR Hub. Add a new class at the root of the project and name it "**LeaderboardHub.cs**". Replace the default generated code with the following code:

```
using Microsoft.AspNet.SignalR;

namespace MemoryGame.Web
{
    public class LeaderboardHub : Hub
    {
        public static void Broadcast()
        {
            IHubContext context = GlobalHost
                                  .ConnectionManager
                                  .GetHubContext<LeaderboardHub>();

            context.Clients.All.displayLeaderBoard();
        }
    }
}
```

The **LeaderboardHub** inherits the Hub class and contains a static class called Broadcast.

The **Hub** is the centerpiece of the **SignalR**. Similar to the concept of **Controller** in ASP.NET MVC, a **Hub** is responsible for receiving input and generating the output to the client.

To make it clearer, the following class:

```
public class LeaderboardHub : Hub
```

will generate the following JavaScript client proxy:

```
var hubProxy = $.connection.leaderboardHub;
```

By default, JavaScript clients refer to Hubs by using a camel-cased version of the class name. SignalR automatically makes this change so that JavaScript code can conform to JavaScript conventions. The preceding example code would be referred to as **leaderBoardHub** in JavaScript code. We'll take a look at how we are going to invoke the Hub from our JavaScript code later in this chapter.

The **Broadcast()** method creates an instance of the IHubContext interface. **IHubContext** provides access to information about an **IHub** and basically exposes two main properties, which are the **Clients** and **Groups**. In this example, a connected client can call the **Broadcast** server method and **displayLeaderBoard** client proxy method, and when it does, the data received is broadcast to all connected clients, as shown in the following figure:

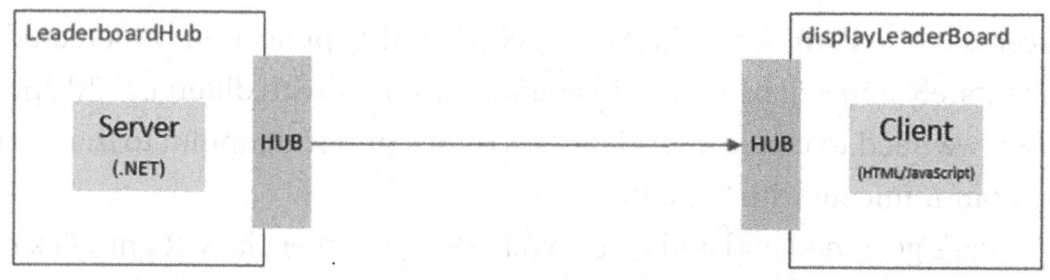

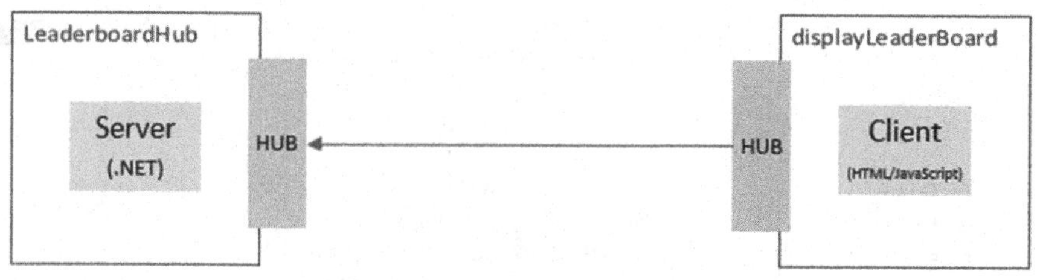

Figure 5-8. *SignalR client-to-server invocation and vice versa*

SignalR handles connection management automatically and lets you broadcast messages to all connected clients simultaneously, like a chat room. You can also send messages to specific clients. The connection between the client and server is persistent, unlike a classic HTTP connection, which is re-established for each communication.

SignalR provides a simple API for creating server-to-client remote procedure calls (RPC) that call JavaScript functions in client browsers (and other client platforms) from server-side .NET code. SignalR also includes API for connection management (for instance, connect and disconnect events) and grouping connections.

Adding an API Endpoint

At this point, the **MemoryGame.API** Web API server doesn't have access to the **Hub**. Since the MemoryGame.API application was created separately and will be hosted in a different server with different URL/ports, then we need to create an API for exposing a public endpoint to that server to communicate with SignalR.

Let's go ahead and add a new Web API controller class. Right-click the **Controllers** folder and then select **Add ➤ Web API Controller class (v2.1)** as shown in the following figure:

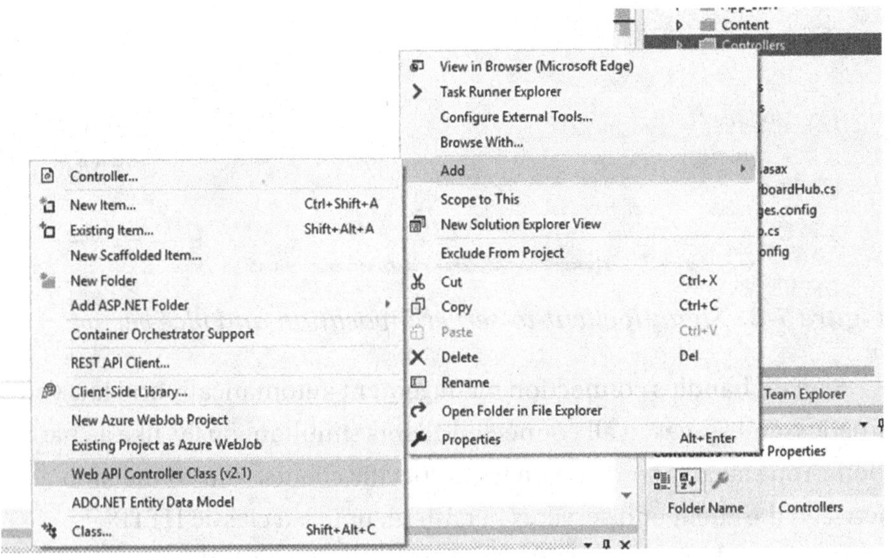

Figure 5-9. Adding a new Web API controller class

On the next screen, name the class "**LeaderBoardAppController**", just like in the following figure:

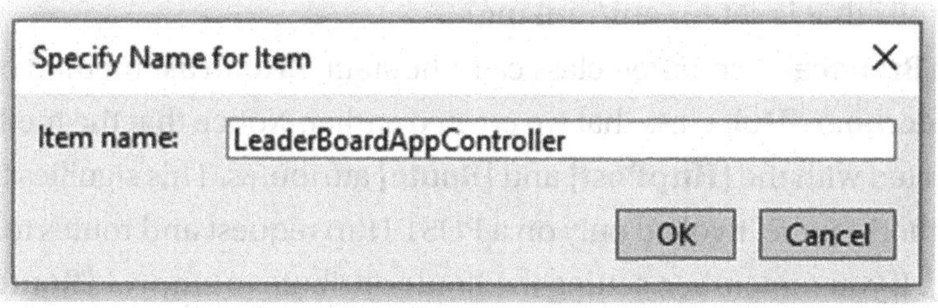

Figure 5-10. Setting a controller name

Click **OK** and then replace the default generated code with the following code:

```
using System.Web.Http;

namespace MemoryGame.Web.Controllers
{
    [RoutePrefix("api/ranking")]
    public class LeaderBoardAppController : ApiController
    {
        [HttpPost,Route("")]
        public void Broadcast()
        {
            LeaderboardHub.Broadcast();
        }
    }
}
```

The **LeaderBoardAppController** class derives the **ApiController** class, which enables it to become a Web API controller rather an MVC controller. This class uses the **RoutePrefix** attribute to define a common route prefix that is set to "api/ranking".

The **Broadcast()** method class calls the static **Broadcast** method of the **LeaderboardHub** class that we created earlier. Notice that the method is decorated with the **[HttpPost]** and **[Route]** attributes. This signifies that this method can be invoked only on a POST Http request and routes to "api/ranking". If you remember, setting the Route attribute to empty (**[Route("")]**) automatically maps to the base route defined at the class level.

Note You can also define a client proxy method outside the Hub via IHubContext. For example, in your Web API controller action, you can do something like in the following code:

```
[HttpPost, Route("")]
public void Broadcast()
{
    IHubContext context = GlobalHost
                          .ConnectionManager
                          .GetHubContext<LeaderboardHub>();

    context.Clients.All.displayLeaderBoard();
}
```

Note If you want to use Hubs API for SignalR version 2 in .NET clients, such as Windows Store (WinRT), WPF, Silverlight, and console applications, then see `https://docs.microsoft.com/en-us/aspnet/signalr/overview/guide-to-the-api/hubs-api-guide-net-client`

Configure Web API Routing

The next thing that we are going to do is to configure Web API routing within an ASP.NET MVC application.

Add a new class under the **App_Start** folder of the **MemoryGame.Web** project. Name the class "**WebApiConfig.cs**" and copy the following code:

```
using System.Web.Http;

public static class WebApiConfig
{
    public static void Register(HttpConfiguration config)
    {
        // Web API routes
        config.MapHttpAttributeRoutes();
    }
}
```

The preceding code enables attribute-based routing for Web API.

The final step is to register the **WebApiConfig** class in Global.asax. In the **Application_Start** method of the file **Global.asax.cs** file, add a call to **GlobalConfiguration.Configure()** method; be careful to place it before the call to **RouteConfig.RegisterRoutes(RouteTable.Routes)**:

```
using System.Web.Http;
using System.Web.Mvc;
using System.Web.Routing;

namespace MemoryGame.Web
{
    public class MvcApplication : System.Web.HttpApplication
    {
        protected void Application_Start()
        {
```

```
            AreaRegistration.RegisterAllAreas();
            GlobalConfiguration.Configure(WebApiConfig.
            Register);
            RouteConfig.RegisterRoutes(RouteTable.Routes);
        }
    }
}
```

Again, take note of the registration sequence in your code or the routing won't work properly and you will end up getting an unexpected behavior.

Enabling API Endpoint-to-Endpoint Communication

Now that we're done creating an API endpoint for invoking SignalR communication, we need to modify the **UpdateScore()** method of the **GameController** class in the **MemoryGame.API** application. Head over to **MemoryGame.API** project and drill down to **API ➤ GameController.cs** file, as shown in the following figure:

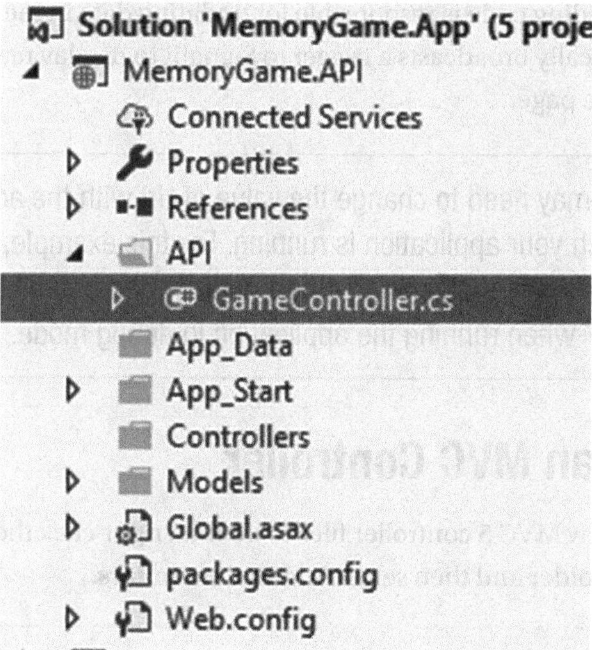

Figure 5-11. *Navigating to the GameContoller class*

Double-click the `GameController.cs` file to open it and then replace the `UpdateScore()` method with this code:

```
[HttpPost, Route("score")]
public void UpdateScore(Rank user)
{
    _gm.UpdateCurrentBest(user);

    HttpClient client = new HttpClient();
    var uri = new Uri($"http://localhost:57865/api/ranking");
    client.PostAsync(uri, null).Wait();

}
```

What we did there is to add the lines of code for invoking the API endpoint that we've created in the previous section using the **HttpClient** object.

The preceding code is responsible for updating data in the database and automatically broadcasts a trigger to SignalR to display real-time live updates in the page.

Note You may need to change the value of Uri with the actual URL at which your application is running. For this example, localhost:57865 is the generated port number generated by Visual Studio 2017 when running the application in debug mode.

Adding an MVC Controller

Let's add a new MVC 5 controller file. To do that, right-click the **Controllers** folder and then select **Add ➤ Controllers**.

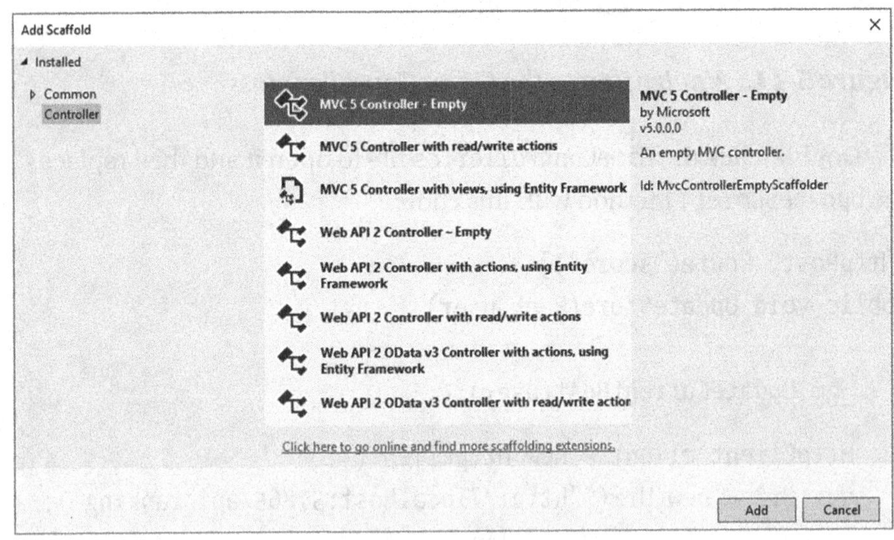

Select **MVC 5 Controller – Empty** and then click **Add**.

On the next screen, set the name as "**HomeController**". Click **Add** and it should generate the following code:

```
using System.Web.Mvc;

namespace MemoryGame.Web.Controllers
{
    public class HomeController : Controller
    {
        public ActionResult Index()
        {
            return View();
        }
    }
}
```

The preceding code is just an action method that throws an **Index** View. For this particular example, we don't really need to build the UI in MVC with Razor, as we will be using only JavaScript and plain HTML to generate the UI. The MVC here is used only to launch a View, and that's it.

Adding a View

Add a new **View** in the "**Views/Home**" folder and name it "**Index**". Replace the generated code with the following code:

```
<div id="body">
    <section class="featured">
        <div class="content-wrapper">
            <hgroup class="title">
                <h1>Leader Board</h1>
            </hgroup>
        </div>
    </section>
```

```
    <section class="content-wrapper main-content clear-fix">
        <h1>
            <span>
                Top Challengers
                <imgsrc="~/Images/goals_256.png"style="width:40px;
                height:60px;"/>
            </span>
        </h1>
        <table id="tblRank" class="table table-striped table-
        condensed table-hover"></table>
    </section>
</div>

@section scripts{
    @Scripts.Render("~/Scripts/jquery.signalR-2.3.0.min.js")
    @Scripts.Render("~/signalr/hubs")

    <script type="text/javascript">
        $(function () {
            var hubProxy = $.connection.leaderboardHub;

            hubProxy.client.displayLeaderBoard = function () {
                LoadResult();
            };

            $.connection.hub.start();
            LoadResult();
        });

        function LoadResult() {
            var $tbl = $("#tblRank");
            $.ajax({
                url: 'http://192.168.0.14:45455/api/game/players',
                type: 'GET',
```

```
                datatype: 'json',
                success: function (data) {
                    if (data.length > 0) {
                        $tbl.empty();
                        $tbl.append('<thead><tr><th>Rank</th>'
                            + '<th></th>'
                            + '<th></th>'
                            + '<th>Best</th>'
                            + '<th>Achieved</th>'
                            + '</tr></thead > ');

                        var rows = [];
                        for (var i = 0; i < data.length; i++) {
                            rows.push('<tbody><tr><td>'
                                + (i + 1).toString() + '</td><td>'
                                + data[i].FirstName + '</td><td>'
                                + data[i].LastName + '</td><td>'
                                + data[i].Best + '</td><td>'
                                + data[i].DateAchieved
                                + '</td></tr></tbody>');
                        }

                        $tbl.append(rows.join(“));
                    }
                }
            });
        }
    </script>
}
```

Take note of the sequence for adding the client script references:

- jQuery
- jQuery.signalR
- /signalr/hub

jQuery should be added first, then the **SignalR Core JavaScript** and finally the **SignalR Hub script**.

The reference to the SignalR-generated proxy is dynamically generated JavaScript code, not a physical file. SignalR creates the JavaScript code for the proxy on the fly and serves it to the client in response to the "/signalr/hubs" URL.

Again, take note of the preceding script's order sequence reference; otherwise, SignalR client will not work.

For more information, see ***`https://docs.microsoft.com/en-us/aspnet/signalr/overview/guide-to-the-api/hubs-api-guide-javascript-client`***

Let's take a look at what we did there by breaking the code into sections.

The **LoadResult()** function uses a jQuery AJAX to invoke a Web API call through AJAX **GET** request. If there's any data from the response, it will generate an HTML by looping through the rows. The **LoadResult()** function will be invoked when the page is loaded or when the **displayLeaderboard()** client proxy method from the **Hub** is invoked. By subscribing to the Hub, ASP.NET SignalR will do the entire complex plumbing for us to do real-time updates without any extra work needed in our side. Thanks, SignalR!

Output

Here's the final output when you deploy and run the project:

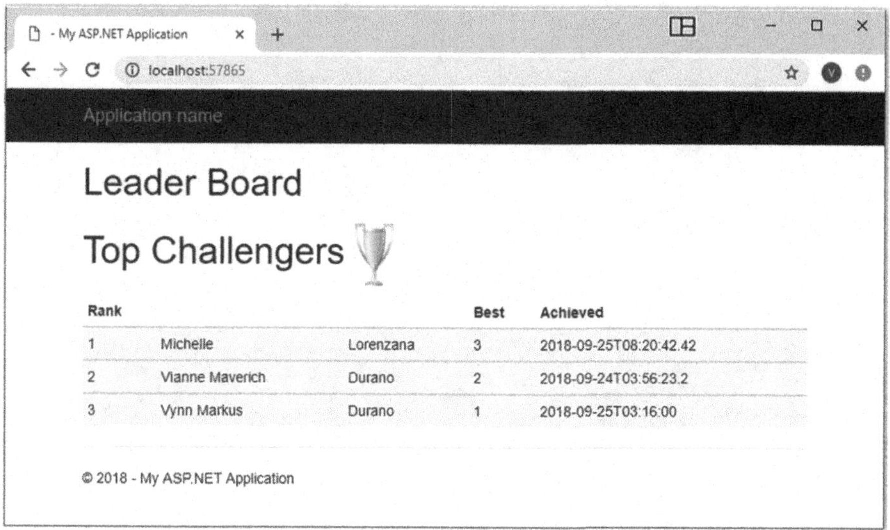

Figure 5-12. *Real-time leaderboard page*

The preceding page uses SignalR Hub client-server communication to automatically update the data without refreshing the page once a user from the mobile app syncs their information and scores.

CHAPTER 6

Deployment and Testing

This chapter discusses how to test and deploy our Xamarin.Android and Xamarin.iOS apps in platform-specific device emulators to simulate the process. During the development stage, it is required to test the functionality of your applications. Visual Studio 2017 is equipped with built-in device emulators to test your application without having the need to use real devices, although it requires a few extra steps to simulate your app in Mac. As long as your machine is properly configured, it should be easy enough to test out your applications in Visual Studio.

Since the mobile application relies on API endpoints to communicate with the data from the database, then the API endpoints should be publicly accessible. Unfortunately, emulators do not have direct access to localhost. This means that your Web API application project should be hosted in a public-facing server or in the cloud, such as with the Azure web app, so virtual device emulators can consume the API endpoints. However, going to that approach to hosting the API publicly can be a big time-waster if we are still at the early stages of the development. This is because any type of change can happen during this stage and we don't want to always push changes to the public-facing serve, plus there's no way for you to debug your code and hit a breakpoint once your application is hosted publicly on a different server or cloud. You may end up relying on your application logs to troubleshoot any issues, which can be a time-consuming pain.

V. M. S. Durano, *Understanding Game Application Development*,
https://doi.org/10.1007/978-1-4842-4264-3_6

To overcome this hurdle, we will use a freely available plug-in or tool to test the application without needing to deploy it publicly on a different staging server or cloud.

Using the Conveyor Plug-in for Visual Studio 2017

Luckily, as mentioned, there's an available plug-in that we can use to access a local hosted web application from various devices emulators. The plug-in is called Conveyor by Keyoti.

What Is Conveyor?

According to the documentation, Conveyor is used to

- Open up IIS Express to allow access over your local network (e.g., access from phones, tablets, and other devices).
- Tunnel a domain name to your machine, so anyone on the web can access your web development project through their browser.
- Fix most 400 Bad Request errors coming from IIS Express.

For more information about this cool plug-in, see ***`https://keyoti.com/blog/open-up-visual-studio-web-projects-for-access-over-the-internet-using-conveyor/`***

Install Conveyor

Let's go ahead and install the Conveyor plug-in by navigating to the Tools menu ➤ Extensions and Updates. On the search bar, type the word "conveyor"; the result will be something like this:

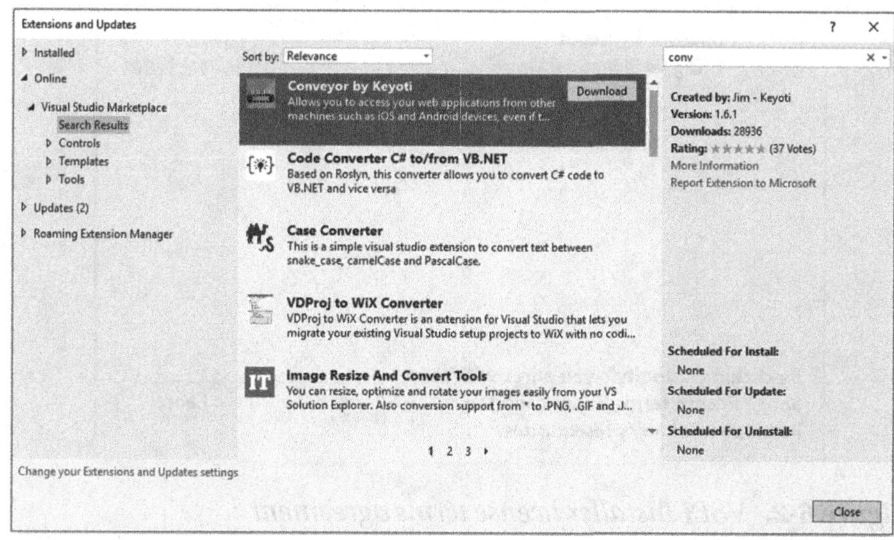

Figure 6-1. *Install Conveyor by Keyoti plug-in*

Click **Download**. You may need close Visual Studio to continue the installation, so make sure to save your work before attempting to install this plug-in.

Once the plug-in is ready to install, it should present you with the following dialog:

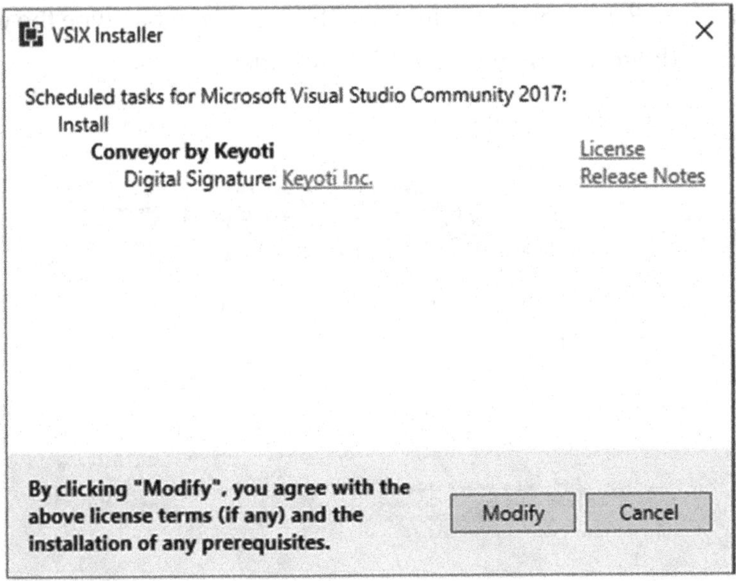

Figure 6-2. *VSIX Installer license terms agreement*

Click **Modify** to start the installation. If you are prompted as shown in the following figure, then just click the **End Tasks** button to close the listed processes.

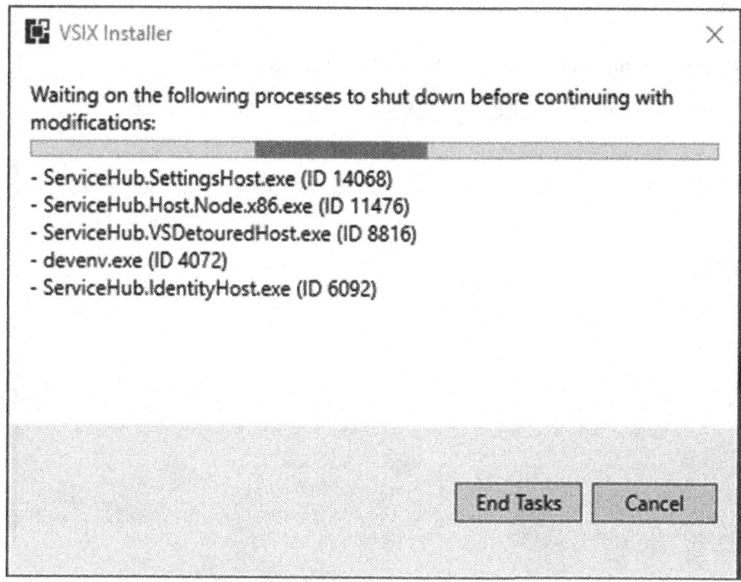

Figure 6-3. *End existing running tasks*

After that, it should then continue the installation as shown in the following figure:

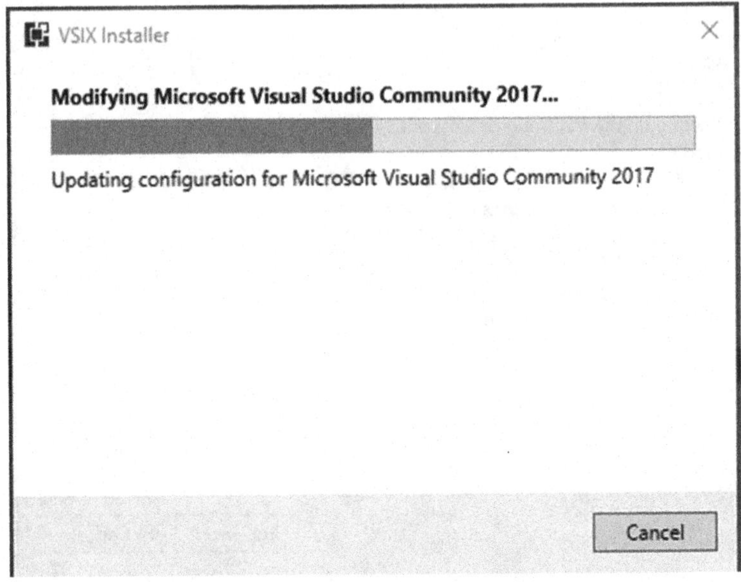

***Figure 6-4.** Modifying Visual Studio 2017 configuration*

When the installation is done, the following information should be displayed:

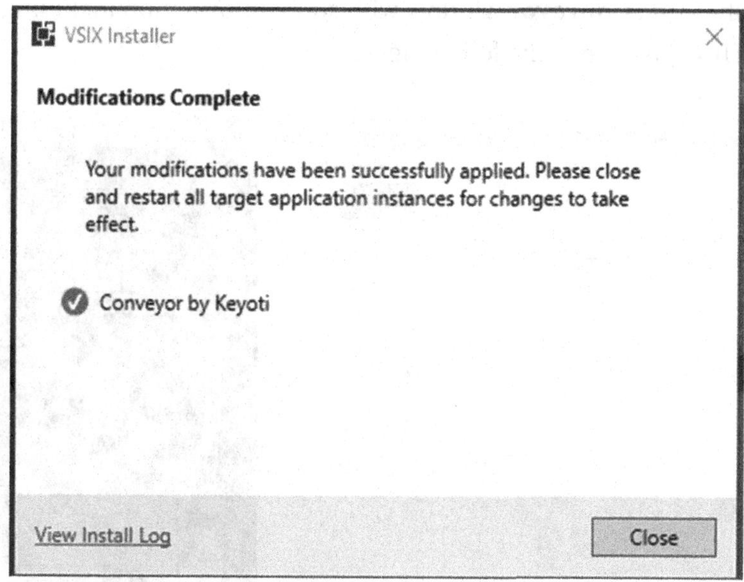

***Figure 6-5.** Modifications complete*

Click **Close** and then follow the next steps to add an inbound firewall rule, allowing access to the TCP port given in the remote URL:

- Navigate to the Windows **Search** bar and type **WF.msc**.
- Click "**Inbound Rules**" on the left pane.
- Click "**New Rules**" on the right pane.
- Choose "**Port**" in the new dialog, then click "**Next**".
- Select **TCP**, enter port **45455** from the **Remote URL** next to "**Specific local ports**", and then click "**Next**".
- **Next**, and **Next** (you may want to disable 'Public'), give it a name like 'Conveyor: WebDev Server Access Enabled.'
- Click **Finish**.

Now, open Visual Studio 2017 and set **MemoryGame.API** as the **Startup Project**. Do a clean and the rebuild, then run the application. It should show the **Conveyor** window with some information including the remote URL, just like in the following figure:

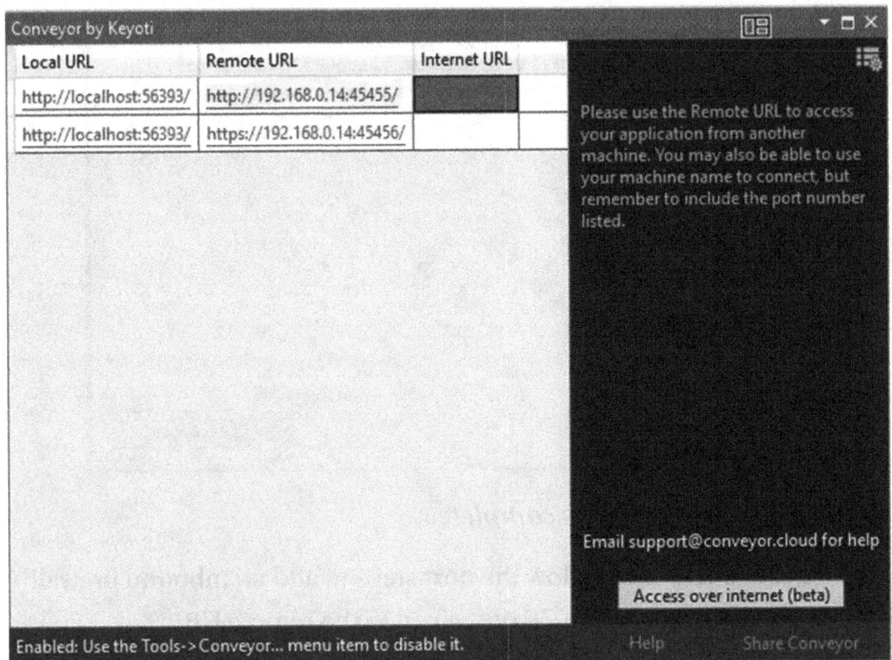

Figure 6-6. *Conveyor UI*

Using the generated remote URL, we can now easily test the mobile application's whole process from different device emulators. All we need to do now is replace the APIUri value from the GameAPI class with the remote URL value.

Copy the **Remote URL** value and stop Visual Studio debugging. Navigate to **MemoryGame.App** project and open the **GameAPI** class under the **REST** folder. Replace the value of the **APIUri** variable with the value of the remote URL you copied earlier. In this example, the value of **APIUri** would now become this:

```
privateconststring APIUri = "http://192.168.0.14:45455/api/
game/players";
```

Using SharpProxy

Another option that you can use to test and debug your mobile applications inside a simulator is a tool called **SharpProxy**. Here's the definition taken from the documentation (`https://github.com/jocull/SharpProxy`):

SharpProxy is a simple proxy server developed with the intent of being able to open up local ASP.NET development servers. This allows you to test, hit breakpoints, and generally do development by using other machines and mobile devices. Simply enter the local port number of your .NET development server and map it with an external port to host on.

Based on the preceding description, it seems like using **SharpProxy** is the easiest way to test and debug the mobile application without doing a lot of configuration. Let's see how it does in action by following a few steps:

- Download **SharpProxy** from `https://github.com/jocull/SharpProxy`
- Unzipp the file, and then run the **SharpProxy** project; it should display the following screen:

Figure 6-7. *SharpProxy UI*

- Navigate to Visual Studio, right-click **MemoryGame.API** on the project, and then select Properties. Click the web item from the left pane and you should see something like this:

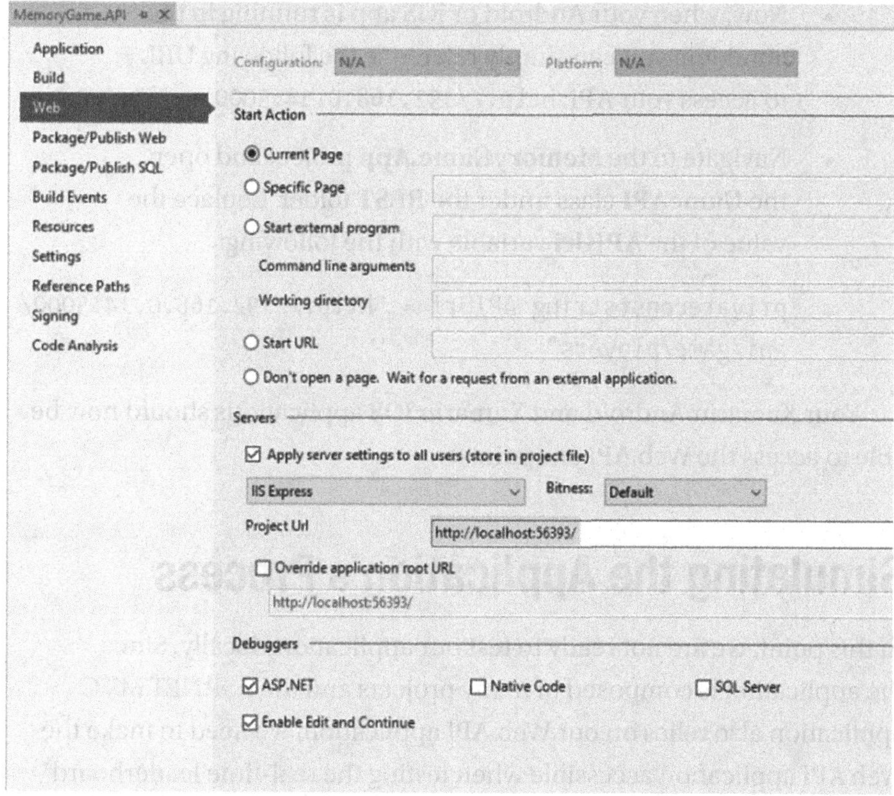

Figure 6-8. *MemoryGame.API property configuration window*

- The **Project Url** field from the preceding figure indicates the local URL where the API should run in debug mode. Take the **56393** value from the URL.
- Enter the **56393** port number in the **Internal Port** field of the SharpProxy UI.
- Copy the **IP Address** generated from the SharpProxy and the **External Port** number. For this example, the values should be **192.168.0.14** for the IP address and **5000** for the external port.

- Now, when your Android or iOS app is running in the emulator, you can simply reference the following URL to access your API: `http://192.168.0.14:5000`
- Navigate to the **MemoryGame.App** project and open the **GameAPI** class under the **REST** folder. Replace the value of the **APIUri** variable with the following:

```
privateconststring APIUri = "http://192.168.0.14:5000/
api/game/players"
```

Your Xamarin.Android and Xamarin.iOS applications should now be able to access the Web API endpoints.

Simulating the Application's Process

At this point, we are not ready to test our applications locally. Since the application is composed of many projects and the ASP.NET.MVC application also relies on our Web API application, we need to make the Web API application accessible when testing the real-time leaderboard page too. Now, you might be asking yourself how to run them altogether at once. Typically, we would host or deploy both projects in the local IIS web server to be able to connect between projects. Luckily, one of the cool features of Visual Studio 2017 is to enable multiple startup projects. This means we could run both our Web API and MVC applications as well as the mobile application together within Visual Studio and be able to test them right away. All you need to do is

- Right-click the **Solution**
- Select **Set Startup Projects**
- Select the **Multiple Startup Projects** radio button

- Select "**Start**" as the action for **MemoryGame.API**, **MemoryGame.Web**, **MemoryGame.App.Android**, and **MemoryGame.App.iOS** projects as shown in the following figure:

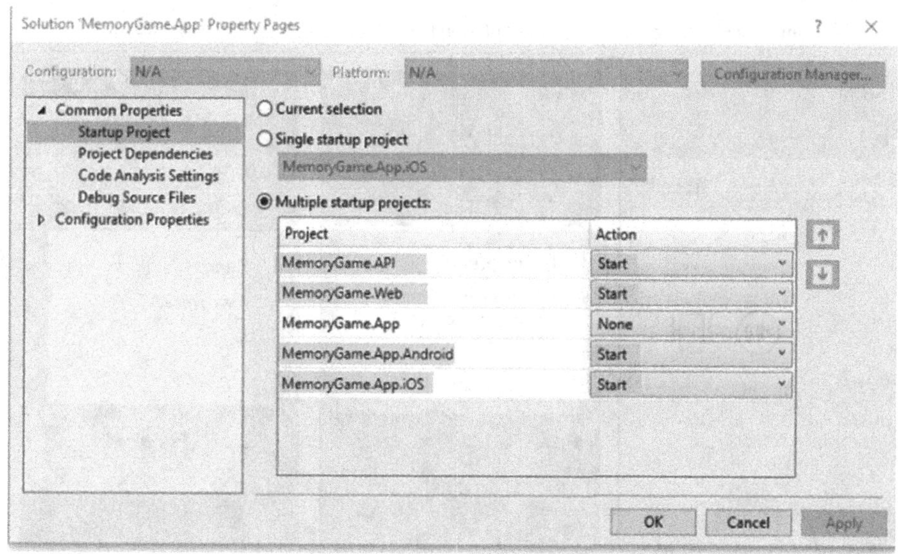

Figure 6-9. *Set multiple startup projects*

- Click Apply and then OK

Now **Build** and press **Ctrl + 5** to run all applications simultaneously.

Android

Here are screenshots of the different views of the Xamarin.Android application that are running within an Android device emulator:

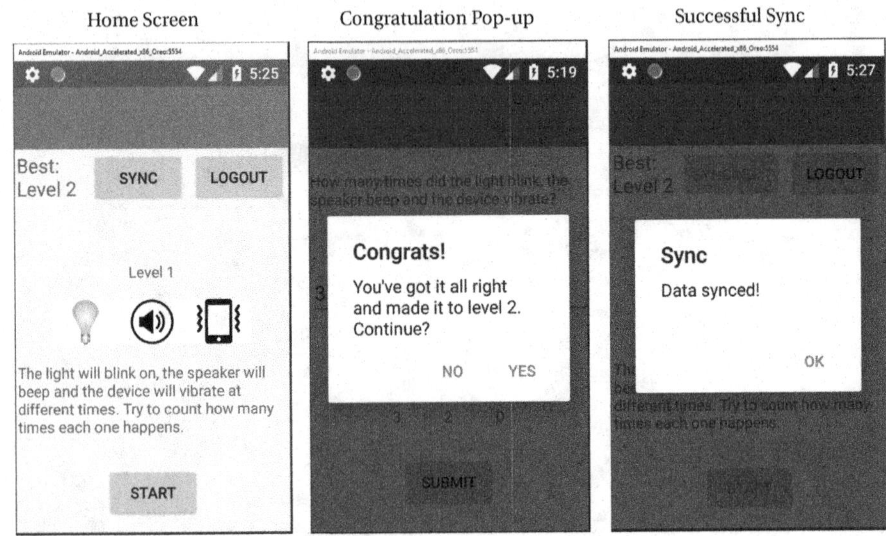

Figure 6-10. *Android device emulator outputs*

iOS

Here are screenshots of the different view scenarios of the Xamarin.iOS application that are running within an iPhone device emulator:

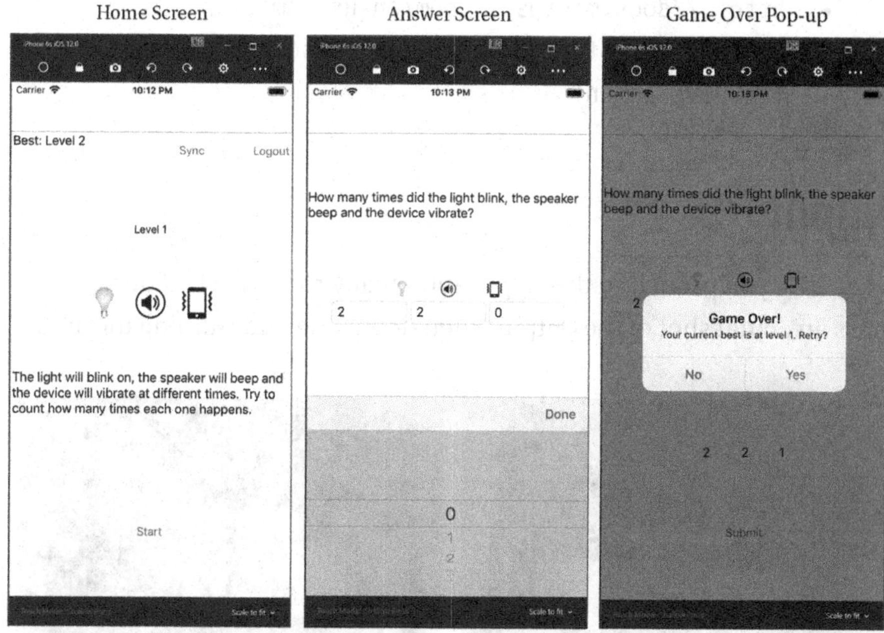

Figure 6-11. *iPhone device simulator outputs*

Next Steps

Simulators are a good place to start deploying, testing, and debugging an application at the early stage of development. However, users will not consume the final application in a simulator, so applications should be tested on real devices early and often. For more information about Android and iOS device provisioning, see the following:

- `https://docs.microsoft.com/en-us/xamarin/ios/get-started/installation/device-provisioning/`
- `https://docs.microsoft.com/en-us/xamarin/android/get-started/installation/set-up-device-for-development`

Output

Just to give you proof that this application really runs on a real device, here's an actual shot of the output when deploying and running the app:

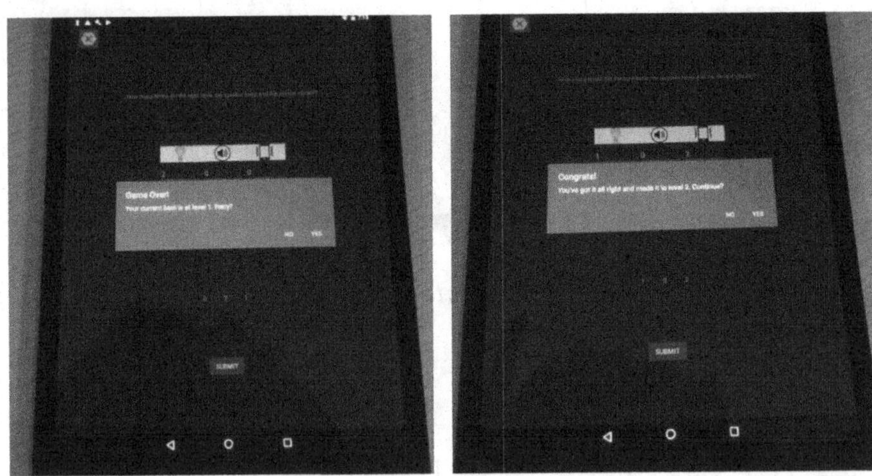

Figure 6-12. *Live output*

CHAPTER 7

Pushing Your Code to GitHub

In software development, securing your code is always a top priority. Unexpected circumstances can occur with your development machine, and of course, you don't want to lose all the hard work and effort that you put in building the software application. Even if you're just building a simple prototype and working alone for a project, you never know when more people might be brought onto the project. Typically, when developing an app, here's a common approach:

- You're working with some new code to get it to work
- You don't want to break your existing code, so you copy your current code to another folder (Folder A) and continue working in Folder B
- If you make a mistake, you just delete Folder B and resume with Folder A

This approach is the idea behind version control. Version control is a process that lets you keep checkpoints of your code so that you can refer back to them if needed.

V. M. S. Durano, *Understanding Game Application Development*,
https://doi.org/10.1007/978-1-4842-4264-3_7

Git is a widely used version control system used to manage code. Code managed with Git is called a Git repository. Also, repos allow you to roll back when you accidentally add something that doesn't work.

This chapter talks about how to push software source code to GitHub. GitHub is a popular hosting service for source code repositories (Git Repo). Here's a brief definition of GitHub from the documentation.

GitHub Inc. is a web-based hosting service for version control using Git. It is mostly used for computer code. It offers all of the distributed version control and source code management (SCM) functionality of Git as well as adding its own features. It provides access control and several collaboration features such as bug tracking, feature requests, task management, and wikis for every project.

Microsoft announced that it reached an agreement to acquire GitHub in June 2018 and closed the purchase at the end of the same year.

Using Visual Studio to Push Source Code in GitHub

The first thing you need to be able to push your code in GitHub is a GitHub account. If don't have one, then you can register here: `https://github.com/join?source=header`

Download GitHub Extension for Visual Studio

In Visual Studio, select Tools ➤ Extensions and Updates. Click the Online tab in the left pane, and it should present you something like this:

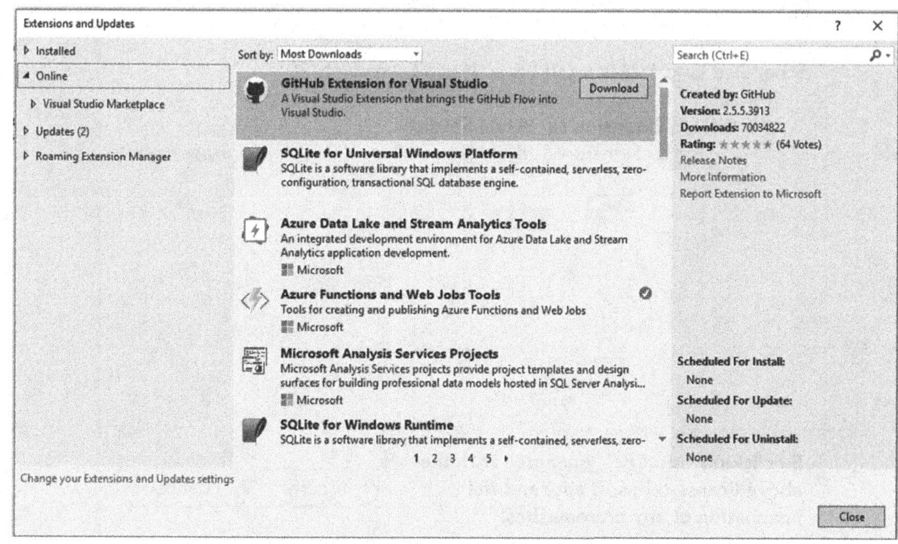

Figure 7-1. *Adding GitHub extension for Visual Studio*

Click **Download**. You may need to reboot Visual Studio to proceed with the installation of the GitHub extension. After a reboot, you will be prompted with the following screen:

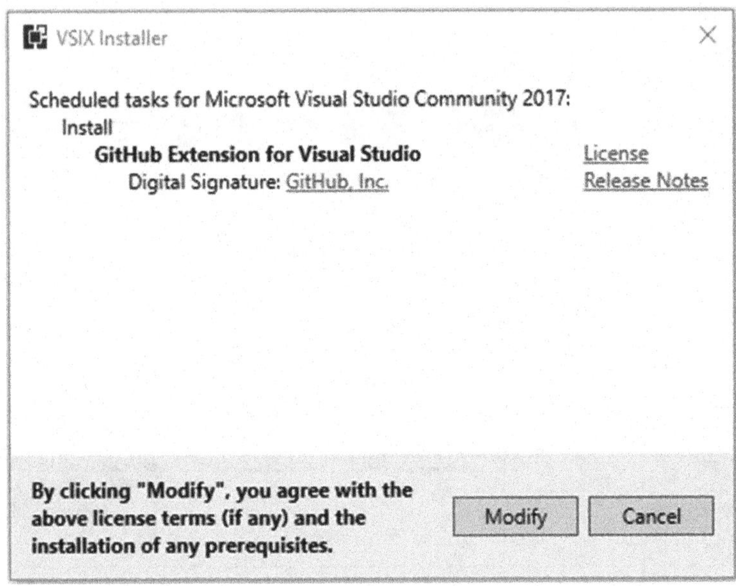

Figure 7-2. *VSIX Installer license terms agreement*

Click **Modify**. You may also be required to end some processes before starting the modification.

Publishing Your Code

After the installation, navigate to the **Team Explorer** panel as shown in the following figure:

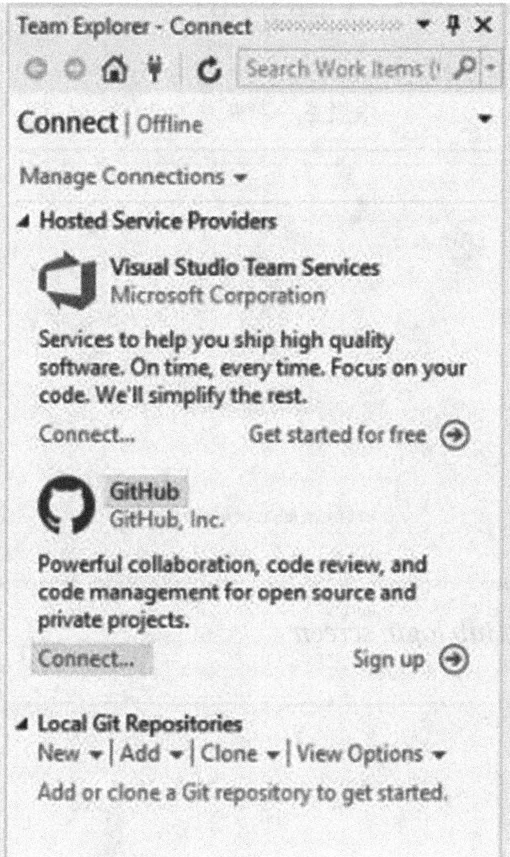

Figure 7-3. *Connecting to GitHub*

Click **Connect,** and you should be presented with the GitHub login screen:

Figure 7-4. *GitHub login screen*

Enter your GitHub account credentials to continue.

On the **Solution Explorer**, right-click the project **Solution** and select **Add Solution to Source Control** just like in the following figure:

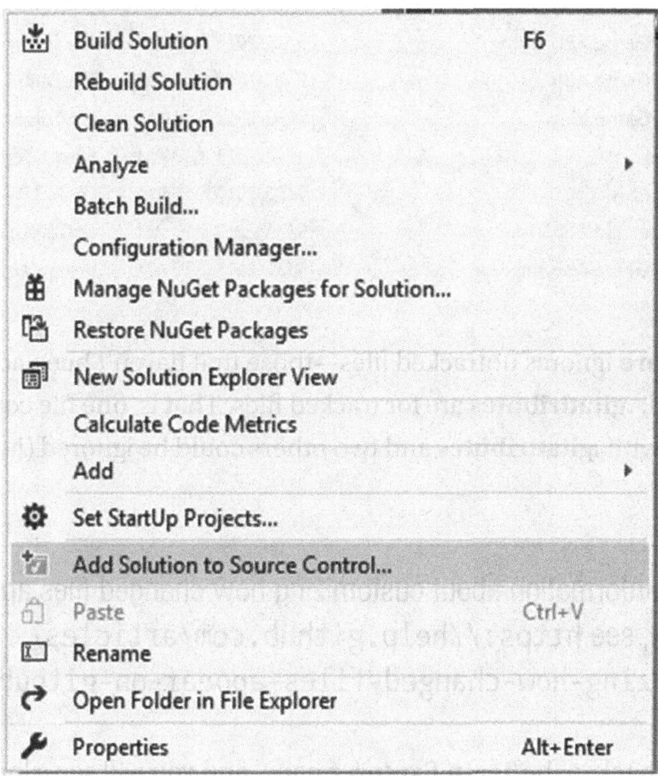

Figure 7-5. *Adding solution to source control*

This action creates a local git repository with .gitattributes and .gitignore files, as shown in the following figure:

Name	Date modified	Type
MemoryGame.API	9/30/2018 4:20 PM	File folder
MemoryGame.App	9/22/2018 6:04 PM	File folder
MemoryGame.Web	9/30/2018 7:04 PM	File folder
packages	9/30/2018 4:20 PM	File folder
.gitattributes	9/30/2018 8:10 PM	GITATTRIBUTES File
.gitignore	9/30/2018 8:10 PM	GITIGNORE File
MemoryGame.App.sln	9/25/2018 2:26 AM	Visual Studio Solu...

.gitignore ignores untracked files—those that haven't been added with git add; **.gitattributes** are for tracked files. That is, one file could be processed with **.gitattributes** and two others could be ignored (just an example).

For more information about customizing how changed files appear on GitHub, see `https://help.github.com/articles/customizing-how-changed-files-appear-on-github/`

Switch back to the **Team Explorer** pane, and you will see a local Git Repository added as shown in the following figure:

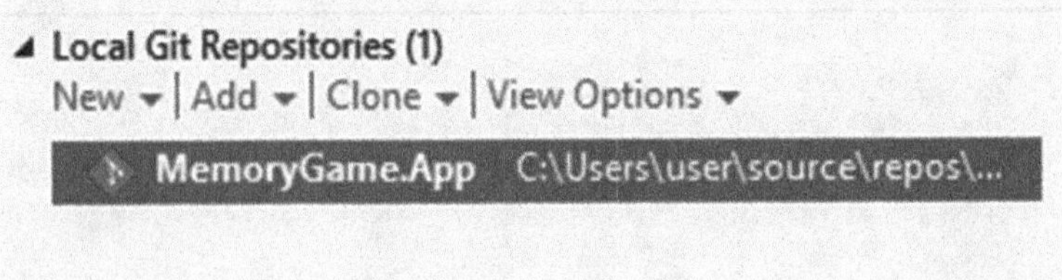

Figure 7-6. *Local Git repositories*

Double-click the **MemoryGame.App** repo, and it should present you with the following screen:

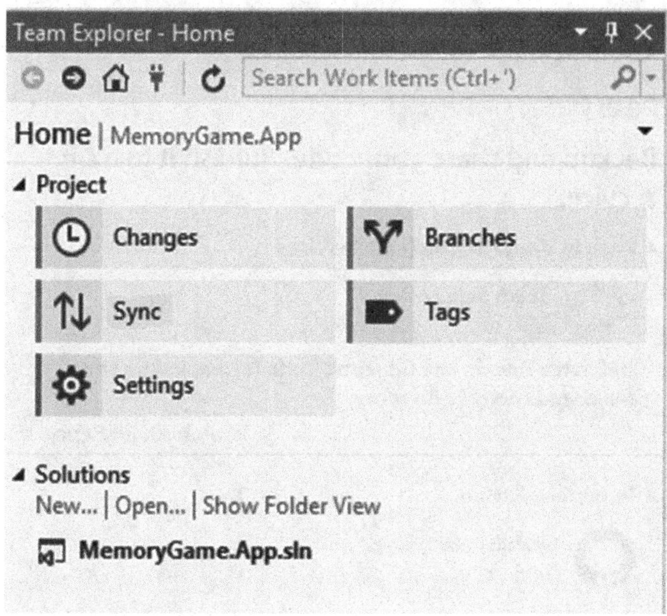

Figure 7-7. *Sync code*

Click **Sync** and it should present you with the following screen:

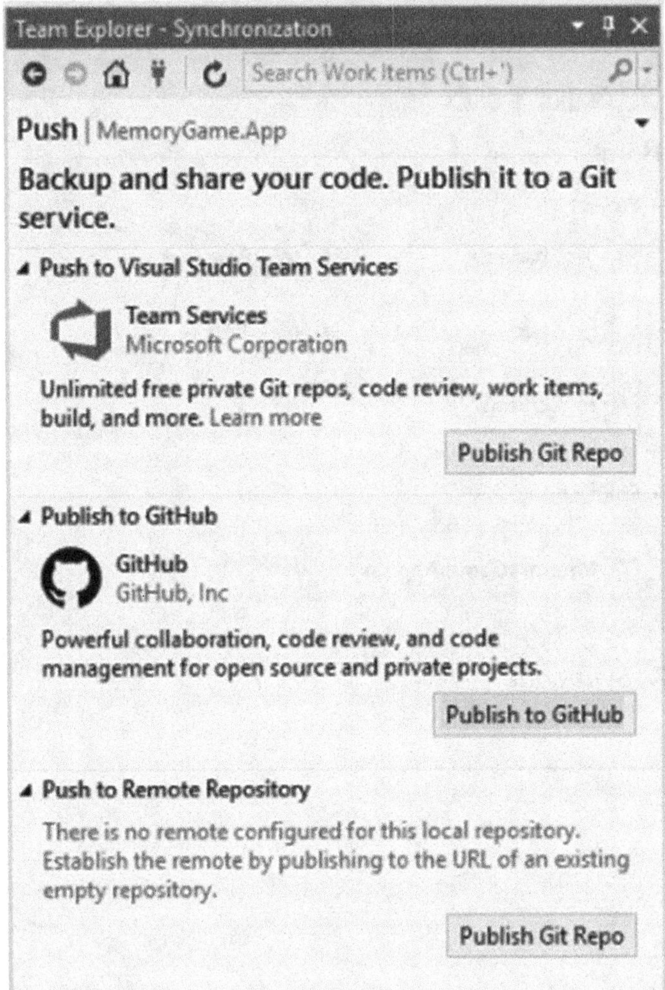

Figure 7-8. *Publish to GitHub*

Click **Publish to GitHub**. On the next screen, enter a **Name** and **Description** for your repository just like in the following figure:

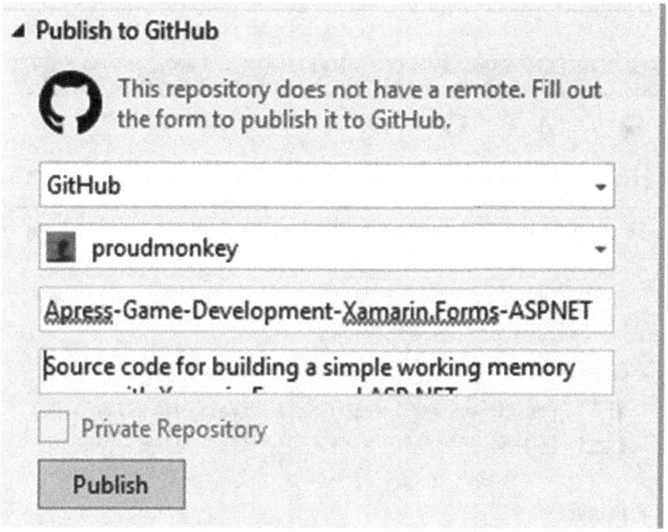

Figure 7-9. *Commit publish*

Click **Publish**.

When successful, it should create an empty GitHub repo to your GitHub account portal as shown in the following figure:

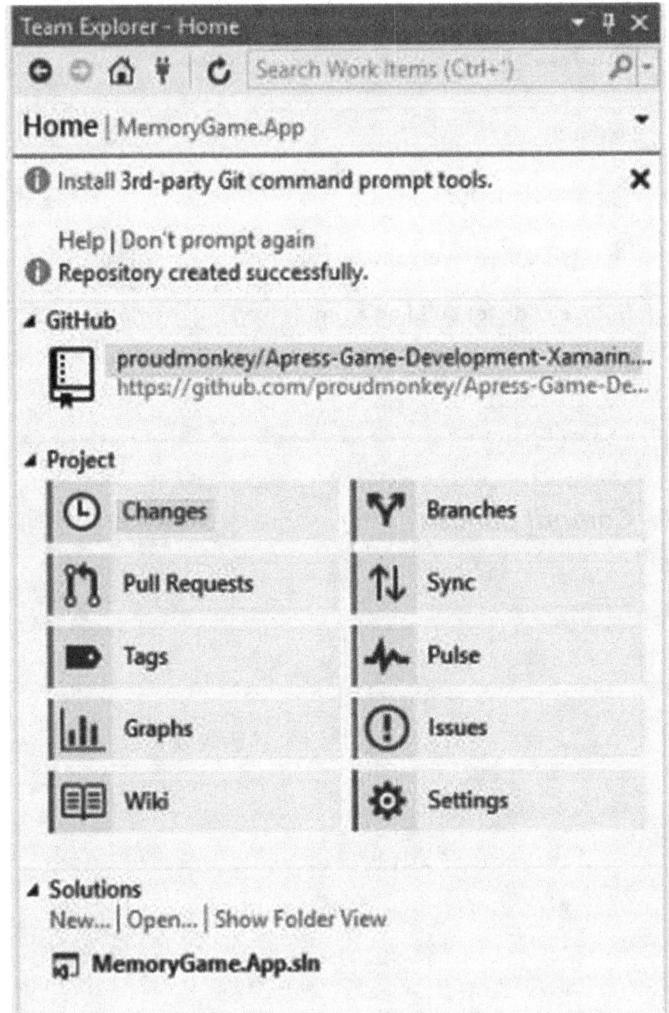

***Figure 7-10.** Repository created successfully*

Click the **Changes** item and you should be presented with this:

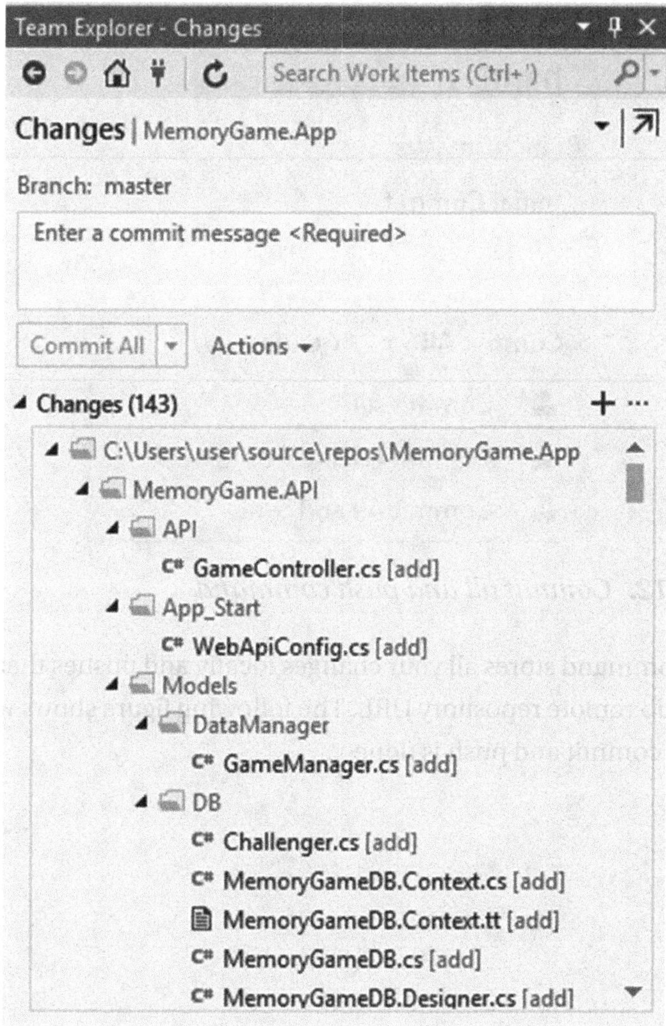

***Figure 7-11.** Enter a commit message*

Enter a message for your first commit and then select **Commit All and Push** as shown in the following figure.

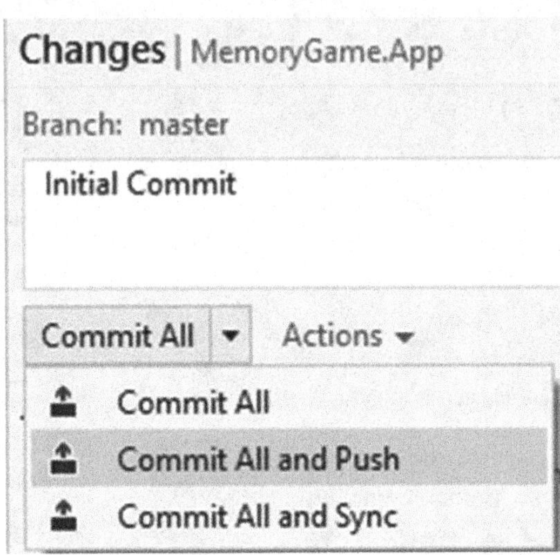

Figure 7-12. *Commit all and push command*

This command stores all your changes locally and pushes them to your GitHub remote repository URL. The following figure shows when a successful commit and push is done.

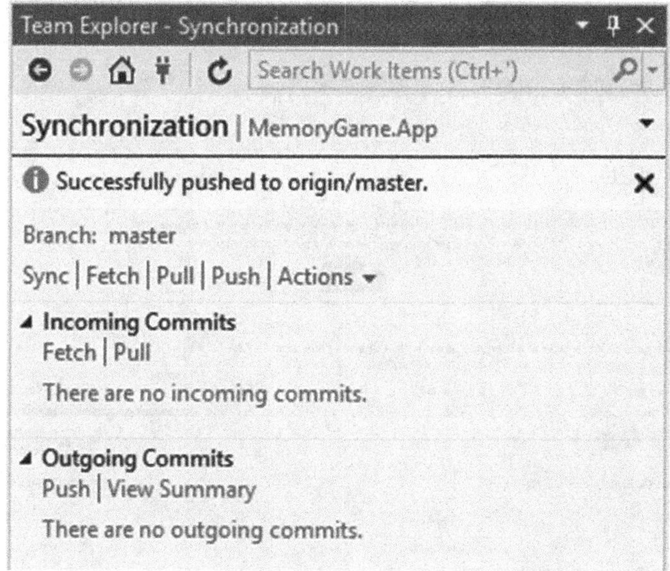

Figure 7-13. *Source code successful pushed to GitHub*

To verify that your changes were really pushed to your GitHub repository account, you can navigate to the GitHub repository URL generated from the previous step. For this example, it generates this remote URL:

```
https://github.com/proudmonkey/Apress-Game-Development-Xamarin.
Forms-ASPNET
```

Here's a screenshot of the source code repository published on GitHub:

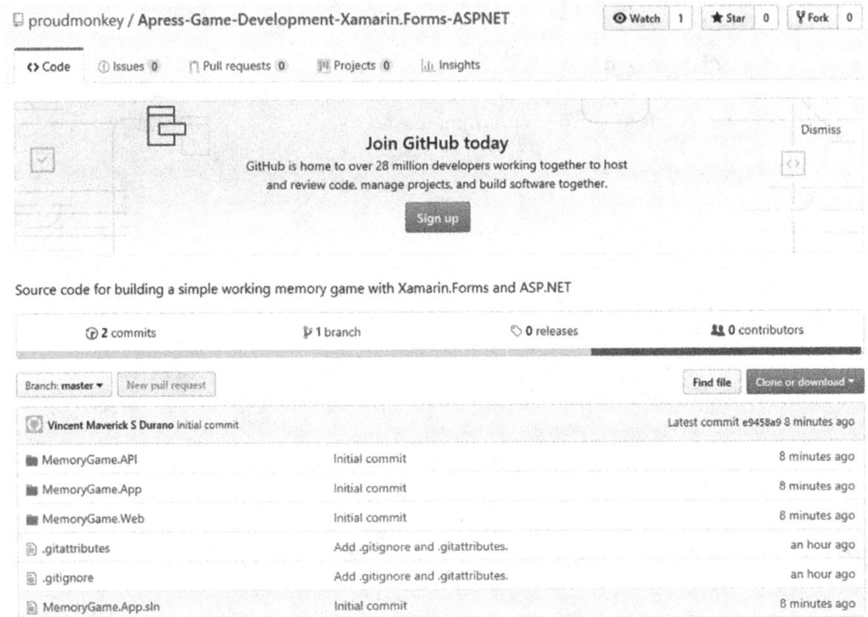

***Figure 7-14.** GitHub public source code repository*

For more information about using GitHub, see `https://guides.github.com/activities/hello-world/`

GitHub Repository and Source Code

You can view and fork the source code here: `https://github.com/proudmonkey/Apress-Game-Development-Xamarin.Forms-ASPNET`

References

Feel free to read more about the topics covered in this book by going through the following references:

- https://en.wikipedia.org/wiki/Working_memory
- https://docs.microsoft.com/en-us/aspnet/web-api/overview/security/enabling-cross-origin-requests-in-web-api
- https://docs.microsoft.com/en-us/aspnet/signalr/overview/guide-to-the-api/hubs-api-guide-server
- https://msdn.microsoft.com/en-us/library/aa937723(v=vs.113).aspx
- www.asp.net/signalr
- https://docs.microsoft.com/en-us/aspnet/signalr/overview/guide-to-the-api/hubs-api-guide-javascript-client
- https://docs.microsoft.com/en-us/visualstudio/install/install-visual-studio?view=vs-2017
- https://en.wikipedia.org/wiki/Microsoft_SQL_Server
- https://developer.telerik.com/topics/mobile-development/what-is-xamarin-forms/
- https://docs.microsoft.com/en-us/ef/ef6/
- https://msdn.microsoft.com/en-us/library/hh833994(v=vs.108).aspx

- https://msdn.microsoft.com/en-us/library/dd381412(v=vs.108).aspx
- https://blogs.msdn.microsoft.com/dotnet/2016/09/26/introducing-net-standard/
- https://docs.microsoft.com/en-us/xamarin/cross-platform/app-fundamentals/pcl?tabs=windows
- https://docs.microsoft.com/en-us/sql/ssms/download-sql-server-management-studio-ssms?view=sql-server-2017
- https://montemagno.com/setting-up-vs-2017-for-xamarin-dev/
- https://docs.microsoft.com/en-us/xamarin/ios/get-started/installation/windows/connecting-to-mac/troubleshooting
- https://docs.microsoft.com/en-us/xamarin/ios/get-started/installation/windows/connecting-to-mac/
- https://docs.microsoft.com/en-us/visualstudio/modeling/code-generation-and-t4-text-templates?view=vs-2017
- https://docs.microsoft.com/en-us/ef/ef6/fundamentals/working-with-dbcontext
- https://docs.microsoft.com/en-us/dotnet/csharp/linq/
- https://docs.microsoft.com/en-us/dotnet/csharp/programming-guide/concepts/linq/basic-linq-query-operations

- https://docs.microsoft.com/en-us/xamarin/xamarin-forms/xaml/xaml-basics/
- https://docs.microsoft.com/en-us/xamarin/xamarin-forms/app-fundamentals/navigation/
- https://docs.microsoft.com/en-us/aspnet/signalr/overview/getting-started/introduction-to-signalr
- https://docs.microsoft.com/en-us/aspnet/web-api/overview/web-api-routing-and-actions/attribute-routing-in-web-api-2
- http://vmsdurano.com/asp-net-core-and-web-api-a-custom-wrapper-for-managing-exceptions-and-consistent-responses/
- https://docs.microsoft.com/en-us/aspnet/web-api/overview/security/enabling-cross-origin-requests-in-web-api
- https://docs.microsoft.com/en-us/dotnet/csharp/programming-guide/statements-expressions-operators/expression-bodied-members
- https://docs.microsoft.com/en-us/aspnet/web-api/overview/advanced/calling-a-web-api-from-a-net-client
- https://docs.microsoft.com/en-us/dotnet/csharp/programming-guide/concepts/async/
- www.infragistics.com/community/blogs/b/brijmishra/posts/building-real-time-application-with-signalr-part-1

- www.red-gate.com/simple-talk/dotnet/asp-net/an-introduction-to-real-time-communication-with-signalr/
- https://help.github.com/articles/customizing-how-changed-files-appear-on-github/

Index

V. M. S. Durano, *Understanding Game Application Development*,
https://doi.org/10.1007/978-1-4842-4264-3

B

C

D

H

I

J, K

L

M

T

U

V

W

X, Y, Z

Printed in the United States
By Bookmasters

Printed in the United States
By Bookmasters